W9-CKT-197

Essential Histories

The Wars of the Barbary Pirates

To the shores of Tripoli: the rise of the US Navy and Marines

Essential Histories

The Wars of the Barbary Pirates

To the shores of Tripoli: the rise of the US Navy and Marines

Gregory Fremont-Barnes

First published in Great Britain in 2006 by Osprey Publishing,
Midland House, West Way, Botley, Oxford OX2 0PH, UK
443 Park Avenue South, New York, NY 10016, USA
E-mail: info@ospreypublishing.com

© 2006 Osprey Publishing Ltd.

All rights reserved. Apart from any fair dealing for the purpose
of private study, research, criticism or review, as permitted under
the Copyright, Designs and Patents Act, 1988, no part of this
publication may be reproduced, stored in a retrieval system, or
transmitted in any form or by any means, electronic, electrical,
chemical, mechanical, optical, photocopying, recording or
otherwise, without the prior written permission of the copyright
owner. Inquiries should be addressed to the Publishers.

A CIP catalog record for this book is available from the
British Library

ISBN-10: 1 84603 030 7
ISBN-13: 978 1 84603 030 7

Design: Ken Vail Graphic Design, Cambridge, UK
Index by Alison Worthington
Typeset in 1 Stone Serif and GillSans Light
Maps by The Map Studio
Originated by United Graphic, Singapore
Printed and bound in China through Bookbuilders

06 07 08 09 10   10 9 8 7 6 5 4 3 2 1

FOR A CATALOG OF ALL BOOKS PUBLISHED BY OSPREY
MILITARY AND AVIATION PLEASE CONTACT:

NORTH AMERICA
Osprey Direct, c/o Random House Distribution Center, 400
Hahn Road, Westminster, MD 21157
E-mail: info@ospreydirect.com

ALL OTHER REGIONS
Osprey Direct UK, P.O. Box 140 Wellingborough, Northants,
NN8 2FA, UK
E-mail: info@ospreydirect.co.uk

www.ospreypublishing.com

Author's note

In conformity with the Oxford English Dictionary, the term
"corsair," which appears throughout this text, may refer either to
a vessel carrying pirates or privateers, or to pirates or privateers
themselves. Readers should also be aware that the
contemporary descriptive term for people and places associated
with Algiers was "Algerine," not "Algerian." Current historiography
continues to use the former.

Note on vessels used by Barbary corsairs

A bewildering variety of ship types were employed in the
Mediterranean, with those most favored by corsairs consisting of
the following:

Caravelle – A small, normally square-rigged, two- or three-masted,
shallow-draught vessel, originally sailed by the Iberian powers in
the 15th and 16th centuries, though still in limited use by the
Barbary States in the early 19th century.

Felucca – A light, fast vessel carrying one or two lateen sails,
usually preferred for coastal or river navigation than for use on
the open sea, with a crew of around 12–24.

Galley – A ship principally propelled by oars, but also rigged with
sails as an alternative form of propulsion.

Galliot – A smaller, lighter version of a galley.

Polacre – A substantial ship with three masts, each constructed
from a single piece of wood with no cross-trees, and carrying a
crew of about 100.

Xebec – A three-masted vessel slightly smaller than a frigate,
whose extensive beam allowed it to carry more sails than other
vessels of its size, and whose unusually shaped narrow hull
featured a prominently overhanging bow and stern. It carried a
crew of several hundred.

Contents

Introduction

Most Americans are unaware that, as a young republic, their nation fought a war with the Barbary pirates, the North African corsairs who plied the waters of the Mediterranean at the turn of the 19th century in search of ships to loot and men to enslave. This is perhaps not surprising, for the wars were conducted on a small scale, over a short period of time, and at a considerable distance from American shores. They were, moreover, the product of one of the most inglorious – even degrading – episodes in the nation's history and, as such, have been conveniently ignored. It is an unpalatable fact long since forgotten, that for many years the new republic paid tribute to the despotic regimes of North Africa in order to protect American citizens from capture at sea. Lacking both the means and the will to protect itself from extortion on a grand scale, the United States – beginning with the administration led by no less than President George Washington himself – furnished ransom payments on a lavish scale. Worse, perhaps, even than a proud nation, whose independence had been so recently purchased in blood, sinking to such depths, was the fact that many of its citizens were forced to wait more than a decade for their release – all the while living on starvation rations in prison hell-holes and forced to break rocks in the quarries of North Africa.

The wars against the Barbary pirates signaled America's determination to throw off its tributary status, liberate its captive citizens, and reassert its right to navigate and trade freely upon the seas. Yet the wars' significance extended beyond this: they played an important part in the early development of America's self-image, its navy, and its foreign policy. When a small party of United States Marines were dispatched "to the shores of Tripoli" as their hymn proudly commemorates, it was the first American military force ever to land on

The frigate *Constitution* leads the American squadron as it commences its attack on Tripoli. Note the distinctive triangular-shaped lateen sails of the corsairs assembled behind the shoals. (Library of Congress Prints and Photographs Division)

a hostile foreign shore, and the planting of the Stars and Stripes on the ramparts of Derna has been immortalized as one of many great feats performed by the Marine Corps since its birth less than a decade earlier. For the Navy, the Barbary Wars became a training ground, with many commanders going on to perform more distinguished service in the War of 1812 against Britain.

The depredations of the Barbary pirates obliged the United States to choose between a policy of appeasement or war. It could continue as a tributary nation or be prepared to defend the right to conduct its burgeoning maritime trade without hindrance. The choice for the young republic was nothing if not stark: to pay tribute and ransom to the Barbary States, so protecting its merchant sailors from captivity and slavery; or confront them – with an uncertain prospect of success – with the very limited naval resources available.

The Barbary States occupied the northern coast of Africa, bounded by the Atlantic to the west, stretching 2,000 miles (3,219km) to Egypt in the east, with the Mediterranean to the north and the Sahara to the south. They consisted, from west to east, of Morocco, Algiers, Tunis, and Tripoli, with Algiers being the most active and powerful of these. Morocco's capital, Tangier, was unique among the Barbary States in bearing a different name from the state itself. All the states were governed ruthlessly by a succession of despotic regimes, with Morocco an independent kingdom and Algiers, Tunis, and Tripoli ostensibly still subordinate to Ottoman authority – though by the 18th century they were effectively independent.

The period of tension that existed between the United States and the Barbary States began only a year after American independence in 1783, and did not draw to a close until 1815, by which time the United States had established the presidency, adopted a constitution, doubled in size, and fought wars with the two most powerful nations in Europe: France (1798–1800) and Britain (1812–15). Open conflict with the

Barbary States occurred on two occasions: the Tripolitan War of 1801–05 and the Algerine War of 1815. In the first instance, the conflict not only triggered a congressional debate concerning the restrictions granted by the Constitution over the powers of the president for waging war; it constituted the first war in which the United States attempted to blockade a foreign port, shell a foreign capital, and land troops on foreign soil. In many ways the Tripolitan War reads like a Hollywood film: on land, a tiny contingent of marines makes a harrowing 500-mile (805km) march across the Libyan desert; at sea, while captive American sailors languish in filthy prisons and endure years of slavery, the infant US Navy engages in bloody encounters over the decks of opposing ships, performing, in one notable instance, perhaps the greatest exploit of the age of fighting sail.

The wars against the Barbary States would provide the US Navy with vital experience that would stand it in good stead during the Anglo-American War of 1812. Indeed, many officers would cut their teeth under Commodore Edward Preble, who led the most successful squadron, later known as the "nursery of the Navy," to the heart of the pirates' lair. Men such as Isaac Hull, Charles Stewart, William Bainbridge, James Lawrence, Thomas Macdonough, David Porter, and Stephen Decatur – all having served in the undeclared naval conflict with France known as the Quasi-War (1798–1800), and all protégés of Preble – would later distinguish themselves in command of their own vessels against the Royal Navy both at sea and on the Great Lakes.

The origins of the wars with the North African corsairs are simple enough to trace. The Barbary States had for centuries partly sustained themselves through piracy. They maintained a more or less constant state of conflict against the smaller, more vulnerable states of (mostly southern) Europe, enslaving their captives and either releasing them upon payment of ransom, or keeping in perpetuity those (usually impoverished fisherman and merchant sailors) whose governments lacked the resources to secure their release. The annual payment of tribute, which varied from nation to nation, protected a country's citizens from capture; failure to satisfy what in today's terms constituted "protection money" left sailors of nearly all nationalities vulnerable to capture at sea, followed by years of hardship and suffering – and not uncommonly death – in captivity.

The pirates of the North African coast shared little in common with their namesakes best known to the Western world – the buccaneers of the late 17th and early 18th centuries who cruised the waters of the Caribbean and the Atlantic seaboard in search of Spanish gold and silver. European pirates such as Bartholomew Roberts and Edward Teach did not, for the most part, conduct their infamous operations at the behest of a government; rather, they preyed on vessels more or less indiscriminately, their object seldom extending beyond seizing cargo and riches irrespective of the nationality of the ships concerned. The Barbary pirates, on the other hand, were subjects of countries engaged in war with other nations – albeit conflict existing merely as a pretext for dispatching corsairs to prey on shipping for the sole purpose of financial gain. In some respects this was not war at all, for the Barbary States had no interest in achieving political advantage over their enemies, nor was the practice of piracy ideological in nature or the product of religious hatred. Raiding commercial vessels was a business – and, indeed, a state-sponsored enterprise – whose limits depended on the vulnerability of the target and the risk of retribution from the nation whose vessels were seized.

Pragmatically, the Barbary States knew better than to intimidate or antagonize powerful nations – that is, those with substantial navies – by harassing their merchant ships. While merchant vessels hailing from weaker nations faced grave risks if they ventured within reach of North African waters, by the time the United States finally confronted Tripoli, vessels flying the Union Jack or the Tricolor stood immune

Stephen Decatur, second in importance only to John Paul Jones in the pantheon of great American naval commanders of the age of fighting sail. "Decatur," said one contemporary, "is an officer of uncommon character, of rare promise, a man of an age, one perhaps not equalled in a million." (US Naval Historical Center)

from seizure. If this was not war on a grand scale, nor was it, from the perspective of the Barbary States, piracy either, for while Western nations viewed the corsairs as mere cut-throats and thieves who took to the seas, the "pirates" styled themselves as privateers sent out legitimately to prey on shipping at the behest of their rulers. The Barbary Wars, in short, blurred numerous boundaries.

Such issues of course meant little to those who fell victim to the corsairs, for prisoners were considered more valuable to the Barbary States than any other commodity. Captives could be exchanged for ransom – and families were known to impoverish themselves for the redemption of a loved one – or, failing this, could be put to hard labor at minimal cost. Over the centuries the institution of white slavery had in fact grown essential to the North African

The Barbary States and southern Europe, 1802

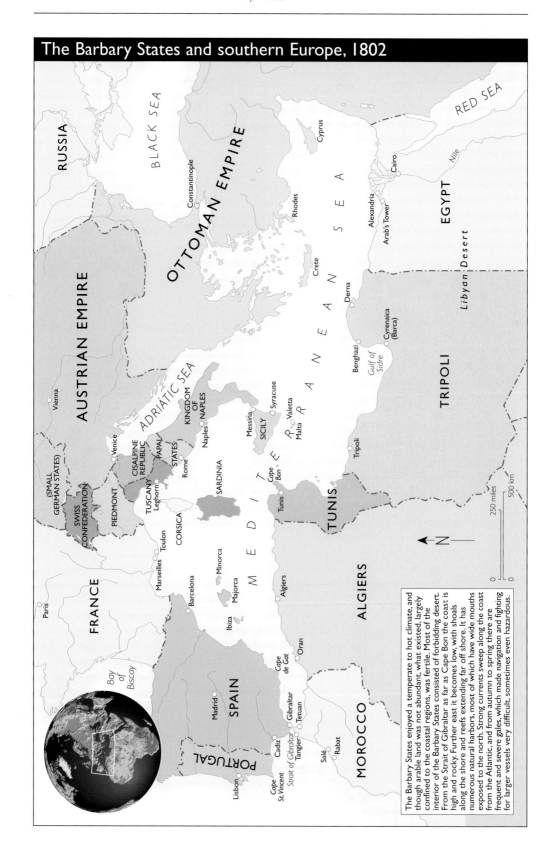

RUSSIA

BLACK SEA

OTTOMAN EMPIRE

Constantinople

RED SEA

Cyprus

Rhodes

Crete

Cairo

Nile

EGYPT

Alexandria

Arab's Tower

Libyan Desert

AUSTRIAN EMPIRE

Vienna

ADRIATIC SEA

Venice

(SMALL GERMAN STATES)

SWISS CONFEDERATION

PIEDMONT

CISALPINE REPUBLIC

TUSCANY

Leghorn

PAPAL STATES

Rome

KINGDOM OF NAPLES

Naples

SARDINIA

CORSICA

Messina

SICILY

Syracuse

Valetta

Malta

Cape Bon

M E D I T E R R A N E A N   S E A

Derna

Cyrenaica (Barca)

Benghazi

Gulf of Sidre

TRIPOLI

Tripoli

Tunis

TUNIS

FRANCE

Paris

Bay of Biscay

Marseilles

Toulon

Minorca

Majorca

Barcelona

Ibiza

Algiers

ALGIERS

SPAIN

Madrid

Cape de Gat

Oran

MOROCCO

Cadiz

Gibraltar

Strait of Gibraltar

Tangier

Tetuan

Salé

Rabat

PORTUGAL

Lisbon

Cape St Vincent

N

0   250 miles

0   500 km

The Barbary States enjoyed a temperate to hot climate, and though arable land was not abundant, what existed, largely confined to the coastal regions, was fertile. Most of the interior of the Barbary States consisted of forbidding desert. From the Strait of Gibraltar as far as Cape Bon the coast is high and rocky. Further east it becomes low, with shoals along the shore and reefs extending far off shore. It has numerous natural harbors, most of which have wide mouths exposed to the north. Strong currents sweep along the coast from the Atlantic, and from autumn to spring there are frequent and severe gales, which made navigation and fighting for larger vessels very difficult, sometimes even hazardous.

The USS *Philadelphia* erupts in flames in Tripoli harbor. (US Naval Historical Center)

economy, and seizing the nationals of Western countries on the high seas proved simpler and more lucrative than obtaining black Africans from beyond the Sahara. The former could be ransomed; the latter could not. Nor, in enslaving Europeans and Americans, was there any risk of capturing co-religionists, whom Muslims refused to hold in bondage.

Captured crews were immediately stripped of their possessions and taken ashore. Some were reserved for service in the ruler's household, but most were brought in manacles to the town square or slave market and sold at public auction or by private sale. Interested buyers inspected a prisoner's teeth and hands, made him run to gauge the level of his fitness, and sometimes struck him to see what reaction he produced. A few

prisoners might be fortunate enough to find themselves ransomed and released within a matter of years, but the majority spent decades – sometimes their entire lives – in miserable captivity. Slaves were often chained together and forced to work in quarries or on the rowing benches of galleys, with death not uncommon from overwork, disease, and maltreatment. Women, though far fewer in number, fared particularly badly, for the most attractive were sent off to Constantinople to serve as concubines for the sultan, while the remainder might find themselves in similar circumstances in the households of local rulers or, worse still, the town's brothels. Still others were doomed to an appalling existence as scullery maids, cleaners, or street vendors.

Many slaves worked on farms, while those condemned to working in government quarries suffered perhaps the most. From dawn to dusk they quarried stone and dragged it into the city on crudely made carts. At night they returned to the *bagnios*,

A North African slave market. By declaring war on nations whose ships they wished to target, the Barbary States believed themselves justified in seizing and enslaving their crews. As such, they rejected the Western attribution of "piracy" to their practices, despite the fact that their victims were almost invariably non-combatants. (Philip Haythornthwaite)

or prisons, there to eat unwholesome and meager rations and to sleep – only to rise before dawn to repeat the whole loathsome process. For years the United States government refused either to ransom or to compel the release of its citizens from this wretched state. Later, it adopted what many contemporaries condemned as the craven policy of paying the Barbary States for protection against piracy. Conflict eventually arose, however, when the United States – bristling with righteous indignation at the continuous demands for more tribute, newly armed with a fledgling navy, and determined no longer to play the role of a tributary nation – dispatched a naval force to the Mediterranean.

Chronology

1778 **April** Morocco recognizes American independence and invites the United States, still in the midst of its War of Independence from Britain, to enter into a peace treaty; formal contact is not made until early 1783.

1783 **September 3** Britain recognizes the independence of the United States by the Treaty of Paris; American vessels cease to enjoy Royal Navy protection at sea.

1784 **May 7** Congress instructs commissioners to begin negotiations with Morocco.
October 11 Moroccan corsair seizes the merchant ship *Betsey*, taking the vessel and crew to Tangier.

1785 **March 11** Congress appropriates $80,000 to conclude treaties with all four Barbary States.
July 9 Emperor of Morocco restores the *Betsey*, her crew, and cargo.
July 25 Algerine corsair seizes schooner *Maria* off the Portuguese coast; the dey declares war on the United States and ultimately demands nearly $1 million for peace; a week after taking the *Maria*, Algerines seize the *Dauphin*.

1786 **March 25** American diplomats arrive in Algiers, where the dey holds approximately 1,500 white slaves, including 21 Americans; negotiations fail, and notwithstanding sporadic talks and numerous delays, are not renewed in earnest until early 1792.
June 23 Morocco concludes a treaty of peace and commerce with the United States.

1789 **April** George Washington becomes the first president of the United States, serving two terms until early 1797.

1792 **February 22** Seven years after the first Americans are imprisoned in Algiers, Congress again appoints a representative to treat with the dey.
April 20 France declares war on Austria, opening the French Revolutionary Wars, which eventually involve most of Europe and continue until March 1802.

1793 **October 25** Algerine pirates capture the American brig *Polly*, and by the end of November ten other American ships fall into their hands, bringing the total number of American captives to 119.

1794 **March 20** Congress allocates over $1 million for the construction of six frigates. President Washington approves this on the 27th, marking the birth of the US Navy.

1795 **September 5** United States and Algiers conclude a treaty of peace at enormous cost to the former; 85 surviving American prisoners from the original 119 are to be released, but America's inability to meet its obligations delays the release of the captives until the following year.

1796 **July 11** Algiers releases the 85 surviving American prisoners in its hands, some of these having spent 10 years in slavery.
August Tripolitan corsairs seize the American merchantmen *Sophia* and *Betsy*, releasing the first, but enslaving the crew of the second and converting the prize into a corsair.
November 4 Treaty of peace between the United States and Tripoli.

1797 **March** John Adams becomes the second president of the United States.
May President Adams asks Congress to arm merchantmen, to prepare the

three newly constructed frigates for service, and to allocate funds to build three more warships; the *United States*, *Constellation*, and *Constitution* are launched later that year.

August 28 Tunis and the United States conclude a treaty, the last of the treaties America had signed with the four Barbary States since 1784.

1798   **April 27** Congress appropriates funds for the purchase or construction of up to 12 warships; three days later it creates the Department of the Navy.

November Hostilities begin between the United States and France in what is known as the Quasi-War; operations are confined to ship-to-ship actions in the Atlantic and West Indies.

1800   **April** Tripoli threatens war within six months if its financial demands on the United States go unfulfilled.

July The 18-gun Tripolitan polacre *Tripolino* captures the American brig *Catherine*; the pasha releases the crew in October but demands annual tribute similar to that already being provided by the United States to Algiers.

September Commodore William Bainbridge, in the *United States*, sails into Algiers with a late tribute payment for the dey.

September 30 Treaty of Mortefontaine ends the Quasi-War between America and France, by which time the US Navy has rapidly expanded.

October Tripoli releases the *Catherine* and her crew, but warns that it will declare war on the United States within six months in the absence of a treaty; on the 19th, Bainbridge sails under humiliating circumstances for Constantinople, bearing gifts from the dey of Algiers to the sultan.

1801   **February 26** Tripoli declares war on the United States, the American government having refused to meet the pasha's demands; a few weeks

later Thomas Jefferson takes office as the third US president.

July 24 Commodore Richard Dale, commanding the first US naval squadron to the Mediterranean, begins the blockade of Tripoli.

August 1 In the first naval encounter of the Tripolitan War, the schooner USS *Enterprise* captures the 14-gun cruiser *Tripoli*.

1802   **April 27** Commodore Richard Morris, Dale's successor, leaves Virginia in command of the second American squadron dispatched to the Mediterranean.

June 17 Tripolitan corsairs capture the American merchant ship *Franklin*.

June 19 Morocco declares war on the United States.

1803   **May 13** USS *John Adams* captures the 28-gun Moroccan warship *Meshuda*.

May 18 Britain declares war on France, marking the renewal of the Anglo-French conflict that had begun in 1793 and had ended in 1802; most of Europe is eventually engulfed in the course of the Napoleonic Wars (1803–15).

June 2 Captain David Porter conducts a raid on Tripoli harbor, the first American amphibious landing on a hostile foreign shore.

June 7 Morris conducts abortive negotiations with Tripoli.

September Commodore Edward Preble, leading the third American squadron to the Mediterranean, arrives off Tripoli.

October 31 The USS *Philadelphia* runs aground in Tripoli harbor and is captured, along with Bainbridge and his crew of 307.

1804   **February 16** Captain Stephen Decatur, leading 75 volunteers aboard the ketch *Intrepid*, enters Tripoli harbor under cover of darkness, sets fire to the *Philadelphia*, and escapes.

August 3 Preble launches a series of attacks on Tripolitan ships and harbor defenses.

August 7, 25; September 3 Preble conducts further attacks on Tripoli.

September 4 The *Intrepid*, converted into an explosion vessel, blows up prematurely in Tripoli harbor.

September 9 Commodore Samuel Barron, commanding the fourth American squadron dispatched to the Mediterranean, arrives off Tripoli.

1805   **February 23** William Eaton and Hamet Karamanli, meeting in Egypt, agree to lead an overland expedition against the port of Derna as part of a campaign to take Tripoli and overthrow the pasha.

March 8 Expedition leaves Alexandria for Derna.

April 28 Arab and American force storms and captures Derna (not, as popularly believed, on the 27th).

June 4 United States and Tripoli conclude peace.

1812   **June 18** United States declares war on Britain; theaters of war will include the American-Canadian border, the Great Lakes, the Atlantic, Chesapeake Bay, and the Gulf coast.

1814   **December 24** United States and Britain conclude peace at Ghent, agreeing to terms that effectively re-establish the *status quo ante bellum*.

1815   **March 2** Released from conflict with Britain, the United States declares war on Algiers.

May 20 Decatur departs from New York with a squadron bound for the Mediterranean.

June 17 USS *Guerrière* captures the Algerine ship *Mashouda*, taking over 400 prisoners.

June 28 Decatur arrives off Algiers, threatening imminent bombardment; a treaty is concluded two days later, after which Decatur proceeds to Tunis and Tripoli, compelling those powers also to conclude peace.

1816   **March 24** Admiral Lord Exmouth, with a powerful Royal Navy squadron, appears off Algiers and ransoms various European prisoners on behalf of their governments.

April 17 Exmouth arrives at Tunis, where he pays ransom for the release of European prisoners held there; he then proceeds to Tripoli and repeats the process.

July 24 Exmouth leaves Portsmouth with a powerful squadron to compel Algiers to release all foreign captives and to abolish white slavery.

August 27 Exmouth's Anglo-Dutch force bombards Algiers; on the following day, the dey releases all remaining "Christian" prisoners.

1830   **June 13** Large French expeditionary force anchors on the Algerine coast at Sidi Ferruch, marking the beginning of the conquest of North Africa.

July 5 Algiers capitulates to the French.

Historical origins

North African piracy had existed for centuries before the Americas were even known to Europeans. Cervantes, author of *Don Quixote*, was amongst those who became a prisoner of the Barbary States, as was, over a hundred years later, Daniel Defoe, of *Robinson Crusoe* fame. The Barbary States derived their name from a Greek term that described non-Greeks as "barbarians," and came to be applied to the nomadic peoples of North Africa, the Berbers. By early modern times the Barbary States consisted of four political entities: from west to east, Morocco, Algiers, Tunis, and Tripoli, roughly equivalent to the modern states of Morocco, Algeria, Tunisia, and Libya, respectively. These territories formed part of the vast and sprawling Ottoman Empire, led by a succession of sultans, with Turkey at its heart and Constantinople its capital – a complex of vast palaces and mosques, surrounded by miles of narrow, squalid streets. The Ottomans conquered North Africa in the 7th century, spreading the Muslim religion and reaching Gibraltar by 710.

Yet while Islam remained a permanent and deeply rooted feature of this region, the political connections between the Barbary States and the sultan gradually weakened over time, a consequence largely of distance and primitive means of communication. Notwithstanding easy access to the sea, the authorities in Constantinople found it increasingly difficult to collect taxes from the empire's far-flung North African provinces. Loosening ties with Constantinople in turn placed the political fates of Barbary rulers more squarely in the hands of local aspirants to power; thus, the peaceful – not to mention predictable – transfer of the political reins from one regime to the next could not be taken for granted.

As a result, the sultan and his ministers frequently found themselves having to cope with a succession of new provincial leaders whose loyalty often shifted according to the extent to which they felt they could exercise a degree of autonomy without risking their heads. In short, the rulers of the Barbary States – titled variously as dey (Algiers), bey (Tunis), pasha, or bashaw (Tripoli), and emperor (Morocco) – often took power by violent means, normally through assassination and coup. They thus ruled amidst an atmosphere of suspicion, fear, and repression, ever-vigilant lest they fall victim to a conspiracy in which strangulation ended one regime to make way for the next. Such men, living tenuous political existences, had in fact much less to fear from Constantinople than from treacherous courtiers, ambitious military officers, and jealous siblings.

The Barbary States were situated on the southern Mediterranean littoral, making maritime commerce essential to the existence of a region whose arid hinterland was marked by a conspicuous absence of roads and settled population. The interior landscape was mountainous in some places and entirely flat, sandy, and featureless in others, while many areas were utterly inaccessible. Rulers, whether benign or tyrannical, enforced their authority over the coastal towns and parts of the interior, but the more remote regions to the south could defy the dictates of governments that seldom possessed the power to control their often nomadic subjects, who had enjoyed a relative degree of independence for centuries. The tenuous nature of political power had much to do with the fact that life itself rested on a delicate footing: with arable land a scarce resource, regular supplies of imported food were essential for the sizable populations of cites like Tangier, Tunis, Algiers, and Tripoli.

Muley Hassan, ruler of Tunis in the mid-16th century. (New York Public Library Picture Collection)

Here lay one of the principal explanations for North African piracy: the scarcity of capital as the basis for the generally thriving commercial economies characteristic of Europe and the United States encouraged the Barbary States to acquire specie with which to purchase imported food. Many of these funds were derived from piracy, for seized goods could be sold or consumed, prisoners could be exploited for their labor or ransomed, and tribute could be exacted from foreign governments in exchange for immunity from capture for their hapless merchant seamen. A ruler's continuance in power partly depended on the steady income he derived from tribute and the regular acquisition of goods and people, a system fed on an unwholesome diet of extortion and white slavery.

For centuries the sea played an important role in this structure, for it was principally on the waters of the Mediterranean that the Barbary corsairs preyed, in a desultory fashion, on poorly armed merchant vessels and raided defenseless coastal towns in Spain, Italy, and Greece. Bolder captains ventured into the Atlantic, sometimes going

in search of captives and plunder as far north as Ireland and even Denmark. Those unfortunate enough to find themselves carried away from such places and thrown into slavery pinned their hopes of liberation to their own families, government, or charitable organizations. In the Middle Ages, various religious orders worked for the relief of the sufferings of Christian slaves held in the Barbary States, and sometimes raised enough money to secure their release. In 1199 in Paris priests and monks founded the Order of the Holy Trinity and Redemption of Captives, whose members were called the Fathers of the Redemption, or Mathurians, after the Church of St. Mathurin. The Mathurians established missions and hospitals in the Barbary States, whose rulers generally supported such institutions, for in attracting the attention of European states and the sympathies of the public, they generated ransom money. Priests could also provide food and medicine, and tend to the slaves' spiritual needs – subject of course to the consent of the authorities. If the scale of piracy in the Middle Ages was never very great, this was little consolation for those actually condemned to a life of servitude.

Considerable change took place at the beginning of the 16th century, however, for with the Christian reconquest of Spain – specifically the fall of Granada in 1492 – thousands of Moriscos (Muslims living in Spain) were forced to leave the country and settle in North Africa. The resulting swell in the refugee population, embittered by the loss of their homes and livelihoods, produced a fertile ground for those eager for revenge. With many turning to piracy, the number of corsairs grew as never before.

Europeans did not allow this unwelcome development to go unchecked. Retribution, when it did come, appeared in the form of a naval or military expedition. Spain, Sicily, France, and Britain all sent fleets – and sometimes troops – at various times during the 17th and 18th centuries to confront one or another of the Barbary States. In 1655, for instance, Oliver Cromwell sent Admiral Robert Blake to bombard Tunis with his fleet.

The English frigate *Mary Rose* takes on seven Algerine pirate vessels, 1669. (Public Domain)

Various powers, particularly Spain, Portugal, and England, held territory on the North African coast for extended periods, usually at great expense in men and money, for by establishing a foothold on the southern shores of the Mediterranean, the maritime powers of Europe hoped to regulate, if only to a limited extent, the seaborne traffic of the Barbary States. Portugal, for instance, conquered Tangier and controlled the city for two centuries, but the requirement for a permanent garrison, regularly harassed by the Moors, made this colony a liability from the start, as it consumed much of Portugal's resources and produced very little in return. When, therefore, in 1662 the Portuguese ceded Tangier to England as part of the dowry of the Portuguese princess Catherine, whom Charles II married, the House of Braganza felt itself relieved of a considerable

burden on its treasury and army. Two decades of unremitting fighting and siege wore down the English garrison in turn, and in 1684 the king withdrew the troops, allowing the place to revert to the Moors.

The practice of Barbary piracy might long have been eradicated had not the major European states spent so much of the 16th and 17th centuries engaged in civil and religious wars, and most of the 18th century in major, often far-flung, conflicts in defense or pursuit of empire both within Europe and without. In any event, the Barbary corsairs were never more than a nuisance, and the expense involved in dispatching an expedition large enough to achieve any lasting effect seldom justified the effort. Instead, European states preferred to appease and placate the Barbary States through diplomacy, with some form of tribute generally being agreed in exchange for immunity from harassment and capture for their subjects at sea. However cowardly such a course of action may have appeared to some

An early 17th-century battle between Spanish galleons and heavily armed Barbary galleys. By the 18th century, worn down by corruption and periodic clashes with various European navies, the Barbary States could no longer deploy such impressive naval forces. (Mariners' Museum, Newport News, Virginia)

contemporaries, it was a pragmatic one, for the problem was simply too expensive to solve by straightforward military means. In short, few nations possessed the means to project power well beyond their own borders. By adopting a far simpler approach – by bribing and subsidizing the Barbary States – European powers not only ensured protection for their subjects, but tacitly encouraged the corsairs to prey on those of their commercial competitors who were either unwilling or unable to pursue the same policy of expediency.

While the more powerful European states stood in a strong position to negotiate acceptable terms, the minor states generally fell victim to the pirates, particularly the small countries of the Italian peninsula such as the Papal States, Tuscany, Sardinia, Sicily, and Venice. England (from 1707, Britain) tended to remain on good terms with the Barbary States, backed as it was by a substantial navy which could enforce treaties. Thus, by a treaty of commerce and peace on April 10, 1682, between Charles II and the dey of Algiers, English vessels could "safely come to the Port of Algiers, or any other Port or Places of that Kingdom, there freely to Buy and Sell." They could leave, unhindered, when they liked and could "freely pass the Seas, and Traffick without any Search." In addition, no English subjects could be "Bought or Sold or made Slaves in any part of the Kingdom of Algiers."

Strength alone did not account for Britain's harmonious relationship with the Barbary States. In truth, such powers were useful to Britain. For much of the 18th century Britain was at war with either France or Spain or the two simultaneously, which meant that both its fleet in the

Mediterranean and its garrison at Gibraltar required a constant and reliable source of local supplies. The North African coastal towns of Bona and Tetuan obligingly supplied the Royal Navy with livestock, especially cattle, thus providing the fresh beef to the fleet that would otherwise have to be obtained from Plymouth or Portsmouth across waters menaced by French and Spanish privateers and warships.

Barbary corsairs had in fact been plying the Mediterranean since the fall of the Roman Empire, but their presence only became significant from the beginning of the 16th century, when the Ottomans sought to end the Spanish control of the coast that extended from Morocco in the west to Tripoli in the east. Establishing ports along this stretch of shore offered a much better prospect for protecting their trade in the Mediterranean. This campaign of reconquest was led by two brothers, Aruj and Khayr ad-Din, known as the Barbarossa brothers, so-called from the red color of their beards. Born on the Greek island of Lesbos, the brothers became Muslims and settled in Tunis in 1504. Aruj and Khayr ad-Din became allies of the ruler of Tunis, who provided them with a safe harbor from which to operate in exchange for a fifth of their plunder. With this arrangement, the scale of Barbary piracy entered a new phase, for by it an established political authority provided its open support. These men were no mere "free-booters" out for personal profit as an entirely private enterprise, but were more akin to European privateers, bearing letters of marque from their governments during times of war.

This new breed of pirate was nothing if not bold. Cruising the Mediterranean with a strong fleet in 1504, Aruj encountered a large treasure galley owned by Pope Julius II bound by rowing power for Civita Vecchia near Rome. Pirates were seldom seen so far north, and the vessel, caught unawares, was an easy capture. A second treasure galley was soon spotted; the prisoners from the first ship were stripped of their clothes so that the pirates could masquerade as the

legitimate crew. Tying their own ship astern of the galley to give the impression that the corsair had been taken as a prize, the pirates waited for the other vessel to approach. The trap was then sprung, and the second galley was seized.

Such attacks did not go unanswered. In 1509, Admiral Ximenes led a Spanish expedition to the Moroccan coast, securing Oran for Spain for the next two centuries. The following year, the Spanish took a small island off Algiers, fortified it, named it Peñon de Alger, and proceeded to control traffic in and out of the harbor. The following year Algiers became a tributary of King Ferdinand of Spain, and a crippling 50 percent duty was laid on Algerine imports of woolen goods. Under such strictures, Algiers turned to piracy in order to maintain some degree of economic livelihood. Accordingly, within three years, the Barbarossa brothers' flotilla boasted 12 galliots (small, lighter versions of the galley) armed with cannon, with a fortified base on an island off Tunis. At the cost of his left arm, Aruj then made two unsuccessful attempts to seize Bougie, another Spanish settlement on the North African coast. Undeterred, his ambitions grew: in 1516, leading a force of 5,000 men, Aruj captured Algiers, removed the ruler from power, and assumed it for himself.

These events could no longer go unnoticed by European powers, above all Spain, and in 1518 Charles dispatched 10,000 troops to crush the Barbarossa brothers' forces at Algiers. Aruj and most of his 1,500 men were killed near the River Salado while seeking the safety of the city. Yet the Spanish, failing to profit from their advantage, foolishly withdrew, confident in the belief that the problem of piracy had been eradicated, and thus failed to take Algiers itself. Khayr ad-Din succeeded his brother and sought support not merely from local rulers, but from the sultan himself, Selim I. In return for Khayr ad-Din's loyalty, Selim sent 2,000 men for his use and appointed him governor-general of Algiers. Thus strengthened, Khayr ad-Din retook the Peñon de Alger.

Tunis, c.1670. (New York Public Library Picture Collection)

From this point, North African piracy developed wholesale into a state-sponsored business, with the distant Turks supporting the practice in return for loyalty and tribute. Khayr ad-Din went on to retake a number of towns still under Spanish control near Algiers and expanded his power over the Barbary States of Tunis and Morocco, taking the former in 1534 and ruling them both on behalf of the sultan. The following year, however, the Holy Roman Emperor, Charles V sponsored an expedition of 600 ships under the famous Genoese admiral, Andrea Doria. This impressive force occupied the port of Tunis, and put the city under siege. Khayr ad-Din emerged from the city to confront his opponents, only to find that thousands of Christian slaves had escaped from the citadel and closed the city gates behind him. The Spanish thereupon defeated, though failed to capture, Khayr ad-Din, took the city and, as was customary in siege warfare, sacked it, massacring in the process tens of thousands of men, women, and children and carrying away thousands of others as slaves – during this period Mediterranean slavery was not exclusive to North Africa as it would later become. The Spanish remained in possession of Tunis for several years, and re-established their former control of Tripoli as well.

In 1541, determined to capitalize on his previous exploits and expel the Ottomans from their remaining North African possessions, Charles V dispatched another expedition to the Barbary coast, again under Doria, in this instance against Algiers. Three days after the troops disembarked a hurricane wrecked over 150 vessels of the anchored fleet, leaving the army stranded and facing the dey, Hasan Aga, with a smaller force. The provisions meant for the army were lost in the disaster, and the three-day march to the new anchorage of the surviving vessels took a terrible toll on the troops, many of whom died from exhaustion and exposure. Many more thousands were killed or captured before the remnants reached the safety of the ships and returned to Spain. Fortune having again tipped in his favor, Khayr ad-Din thereafter raided the coasts of Spain, Italy, and Greece. In 1543 he plundered the Italian province of Reggio di Calabria, and kidnapped the governor's 18-year-old daughter, whom he forced to be his wife.

By the time Khayr ad-Din died three years later, Mediterranean piracy was a well-established fact of life for European merchants and, in particular, the helpless inhabitants of seaside towns. Moreover, the decisive defeat of the Ottoman Navy at the battle of Lepanto in 1571 – which thereafter largely confined Ottoman influence to the eastern Mediterranean while leaving the western Mediterranean a European sphere –

Charles V fighting the naval forces of Khayr ad-Din off Tunis, 1535. (Mariners' Museum, Newport News, Virginia)

led to an increased presence of Barbary pirates in the west, for in the wake of its naval disaster Constantinople could exercise but little control over the Barbary States' activities at sea. Exactly a century later, in 1671, Constantinople lost effective political control over Algiers, whose dey ceased thereafter to be appointed by the sultan, but instead achieved power by election amongst his Janissaries.

Admiral Duquesne ransoms up Algerine captives and bombards the capital, June 27, 1683. (PAD5150; National Maritime Museum, London)

Spain was not alone in confronting the menace of Barbary piracy in the early modern period. England dispatched naval expeditions against Algiers in 1620 and against Salé, on the Moroccan coast, in 1637, in both cases securing the release of some white slaves. An even larger expedition, led in 1655 by Admiral Robert Blake, appeared with a fleet before Algiers and Tunis, bombarding both cities. A Dutch fleet under Admiral Michiel de Ruyter secured the release of several hundred slaves from Algiers in 1661, and in 1682 the French under Abraham Duquesne inflicted considerable damage on Algiers. These operations went so far in diminishing pirate activity that the Barbary States never fully recovered their former power, and by the end of the 17th century, the Algerine fleet was down to 25 percent of its former strength. A long hiatus in major punitive operations then followed until 1775, when Count Alexander O'Reilly led a disastrous

Spanish expedition against Algiers. The final European attempt to terminate the scourge of Barbary piracy in the 18th century took place in 1784, when on September 21 a Franco-Spanish fleet under Don Antonio Barcelo bombarded Algiers for ten hours. Barcelo inflicted only limited damage to the fortifications and failed to destroy the corsairs before his allied force was ignominiously driven from the harbor amidst a shower of artillery fire.

This failure to check – much less eradicate – Barbary piracy was to have immediate repercussions for a small, weak, yet vibrant and recently independent nation in possession of a substantial merchant fleet, but absolutely no navy with which to protect it: this, of course, was the young United States of America.

Opposing forces

The Barbary States

Although every Barbary state maintained a large – if perhaps archaically armed – standing force and could call up irregular troops at short notice, only its naval establishment and harbor fortifications played a prominent part in the wars against the Western powers in the early 19th century. Exposed as they all were to the sea, the capital cities of the Barbary States boasted formidable coastal defenses. John Foss, an American captive in Algiers who after his release published *A Journal of the Captivity and Sufferings of John Foss* (1798), described that city as:

… of a quadrangular form … near three miles in circumference, [en]compassed with two walls, about 25 feet distant, and in some places 100 feet in height. The outward wall is defended by upward of 300 brass cannon, and outside the wall is a deep entrenchment 40 feet wide, over which are built bridges at the gates of the city. In the intermediate space between the walls are magazines, for public stores. The Mole of the harbor is about 500 paces in length, extending from the continent to a ledge of rocks, where there are three castles, with large batteries of guns.

Foss' description only touched the surface: a fortified sea front about a mile long protected the town, in which stood a strong citadel. In front of the town, just offshore, lay a heavily fortified island attached to the waterfront by a breakwater in the harbor, which was only open to the south. At the point at which the breakwater joined the island sat the so-called lighthouse battery, containing three tiers of guns extending as far as the mouth of the harbor.

Protecting this on the landward side was the fish-market battery, supplemented by two other batteries, one to the north, the

Algiers, c.1670. (New York Public Library Picture Collection)

other to the south. In the harbor itself lay a varying number of warships which could assist in the defense of the city. Not counting the guns mounted in these vessels, Algiers had about a thousand cannon facing seawards, supported by a large, though indeterminate, garrison, backed by tens of thousands of auxiliaries who could be brought in from the surrounding countryside. Whatever the quality of their gunners, the Algerines could almost certainly replace their losses with relative ease, and they had an ample stock of powder in reserve. Thus, with permanent stone-built fortifications mounting a profusion of heavy ordnance, the defenses of Algiers were formidable indeed. It was from amidst such heavily protected sanctuaries that Barbary corsairs emerged in search of rich pickings.

Apart from the pirate vessels themselves, which were designed entirely for raiding, the fleets of the Barbary States hardly justified the name, for no state possessed more than perhaps a dozen warships at any given time, in all mounting no more than 200 guns. Such craft usually consisted of light and fast brigs and sloops, but might even extend to a more substantial vessel, such as a frigate. Crews varied in size from several dozen to about 400 men for the largest ships. Many Barbary vessels were foreign-built, either prizes taken at sea and refitted, or new ships furnished, paradoxically, by various European tributaries in exchange for peace. Nor did the Barbary States produce much in the way of naval stores of their own. These were normally purchased from European traders, again, perversely, with tribute money or in lieu of it – as with the ships for which the armaments and fittings were intended – extorted from those nations that wished to acquire protection for their merchants innocently engaged in the Mediterranean trade.

Pirate vessels, with crews varying in size from two dozen to as many as 200, usually consisted of caravelles, xebecs, and feluccas: sleek, highly maneuverable, shallow-draught, two- or three-masted craft with lateen sails, which could generally overtake a heavily laden merchantman or evade an enemy warship as their own light armament invariably required. Some corsairs, especially those intended for longer forays into the Atlantic, were square-rigged in the European style, and consequently sometimes escaped

Various North African corsairs. The vessel in the foreground is typical of such craft, which in this example mounts only 14 guns. Pirate tactics favored swiftness, surprise, and boarding, over the application of firepower. (PAD7379; National Maritime Museum, London)

recognition as North African in origin. Oar-powered galleys and galliots had all but disappeared by the 18th century, but the few still in service were, in true medieval tradition, dreadful, stinking, disease-ridden floating death-traps, manned by slaves chained to their benches day and night, sometimes for months at a time.

Corsairs frequently employed deception, often flying false colors – the flag of another, generally neutral, country – to enable them to approach an unsuspecting victim and even lure her closer by feigning a desire to communicate. Writing in 1799, William Eaton, the American consul at Tunis, described the pirates' simple, yet highly effective, tactics:

Their mode of attack is uniformly boarding. For this their vessels are peculiarly constructed. Their long lateen yards drop on board the enemy and afford a safe and easy conveyance for the men who man them for this purpose; but being always crowded with men, they throw them in from all points of the rigging and from all quarters of the decks, having their sabres grasped between their teeth and their loaded pistols in their belts, that they may have the free use of their hands in scaling the gunnels or netting of their enemy. In this mode of attack they are very active and very desperate … Proper defenses against them are high nettings with chains sufficiently strong to prevent their being cut away, buckshot plentifully administered from muskets or blunderbusses, and lances [boarding pikes]. But it is always best to keep them at a distance [so] that advantage may be taken of their ignorance at manoeuvring.

Wielding their characteristic, curved scimitars and instilling panic with their blood-curdling cries, Barbary pirates sometimes subdued their victims with their merciless reputation alone: it was well

Algerine pirates rowing to shore. After the Ottoman defeat at Lepanto in 1571, the Barbary powers found themselves excluded from European markets and bereft of Turkish naval support – both conditions under which piracy would begin to flourish. (Mariners' Museum, Newport News, Virginia)

Hand-to-hand combat with cutlass, scimitar, pistol, and pike. Fighting at close quarters proved a vicious, merciless affair. (Philip Haythornthwaite)

known that these fearsome adversaries gave no quarter to crews who offered resistance to capture. As a result, the men of a defenseless merchant ship, once overtaken by a pirate vessel, generally submitted to their fate; even slavery was preferable to certain death.

The United States

When the United States went to war with Tripoli, its navy had only been in existence a generation, starting life as the Continental Navy on October 13, 1775. Yet by 1785, after only a decade of service and within just two years of the end of the Revolutionary War, every vessel had been sold off by Congress. The Navy, quite simply, ceased to exist. Whereas an army, however ludicrously tiny it was, was maintained for the sake of protecting the frontier against Indian raids, legislators regarded the maintenance of a permanent naval establishment as an extravagance at best and a threat to liberty at worst. Belatedly, Congress only voted for the creation of a standing (i.e. permanent) naval force on March 20, 1794, allocating funds for the construction of six frigates, including the *United States* (44 guns), *Constitution* (44), and *Constellation* (36). These so-called super frigates – being more heavily built than their

counterparts in European navies – were launched between May and October 1797.

These were welcome developments during a period of growing tension between the United States and France, which by July of the following year would be engaged in an undeclared or "Quasi" war that would continue until 1800. The launching of the frigates symbolized for many Americans an end to their growing sense of frustration at the nation's inability to protect its commerce in the Mediterranean and so cast off its costly, not to mention demeaning, tributary status. Congressman Robert Goodloe Harper of South Carolina summed up the opinion of many across the nation who had grown weary of the government's craven policy when he pledged with simple eloquence: "Millions for defense, but not one cent for tribute!"

As conflict with France loomed ever closer, on April 27, 1798, Congress passed an appropriations bill enabling the Navy to acquire through purchase or construction 12 warships to augment its existing modest establishment, though none to exceed 22 guns each. In this effort to assemble a more

Shipwrights are seen here constructing the *Philadelphia*, a 36-gun frigate funded by the people of that city in a patriotic drive to oppose France in the Quasi-War of 1798–1800. (US Naval Historical Center)

respectable naval force, the federal government purchased several merchant vessels and converted them into warships, some in a matter of weeks. By the end of the year the Navy possessed a total of 12 ships fully fitted out for sea, half of these specially constructed for the Navy (including the three super frigates launched the previous year) and the other half being converted merchantmen. To supplement this force, another 14 vessels, including frigates, were under construction. The total manpower available to the Navy stood at about 4,000 officers and men, a number that would continue to rise as new vessels entered the service. Congress also approved the construction of the nation's first ships of the line, to mount 74 guns each, though these were not commissioned for many years to come. The young republic's fitful evolution

towards the creation of a proper navy was at last bearing fruit; it now only needed the political machinery to administer it. Thus, on April 30, only three days after it passed the appropriations bill, Congress created the Department of the Navy and the office of secretary of the navy.

The Quasi-War naturally accelerated the rate of American naval construction, and by the time peace with France was restored in 1800, the United States Navy – newly expanded, battle-tested, and with dozens of French prizes to its credit – was at last in a position to face the Barbary States. Yet, paradoxically, in February 1801 the outgoing Adams administration sought to introduce drastic measures of economy in the Department of the Navy. Congress duly passed the Naval Peace Establishment Bill, authorizing the president to sell off many of the Navy's vessels, apart from 13 frigates and the 12-gun schooner *Enterprise*. Thomas Jefferson entered office the following month, and within three weeks the Department of

The *Philadelphia* cruising off Tripoli in 1803. Formidable though she certainly was in the open sea, this heavy frigate could not negotiate Tripoli harbor without taking careful soundings. The Americans soon discovered to their cost that operations along the rocky coasts of North Africa required more than firepower alone. (Mariners' Museum, Newport News, Virginia)

the Navy had sold 17 vessels. Funds originally appropriated for naval expansion under the previous administration, while hostilities were still underway with France, were simply returned to the Treasury. Six frigates were placed "in ordinary" (laid up out of service pending future need), while the administration, by pursuing a program of gunboat construction, demonstrated its short-sighted preference for coastal defense over offensive capabilities.

When news eventually arrived in Washington that Tripoli had declared war on the United States, Jefferson ceased some of his naval reductions, for the country now required, above all, serviceable frigates to be dispatched thousands of miles from home waters to the Mediterranean. Fortunately for the United States, its naval architects designed the best frigates in the world, the beautifully crafted 44-gun *Constitution* being a prime example of their expertise and ingenuity. Built between 1794 and 1797 in Boston, she measured 204ft (62.2m) long,

50ft (15.2m) longer than a standard British frigate. Her beam, at 43ft 6in (13.3m), was also a yard wider, and her displacement of 2,200 tons (1,995 tonnes) exceeded her Royal Navy counterparts by 25 percent. American materials were superb, for New England was blessed with magnificent forests, which supplied the pine for *Constitution*'s exceptionally strong masts, from which were suspended 42,000 sq. ft (3,864 sq. m) of sail. Her nickname, "Old Ironsides," earned during the War of 1812, was entirely apt for so heavily constructed were her frames – which contained a much greater proportion of timber than a typical frigate – that round shot (cannon balls) would frequently bounce off the vessel's

The United States in 1803

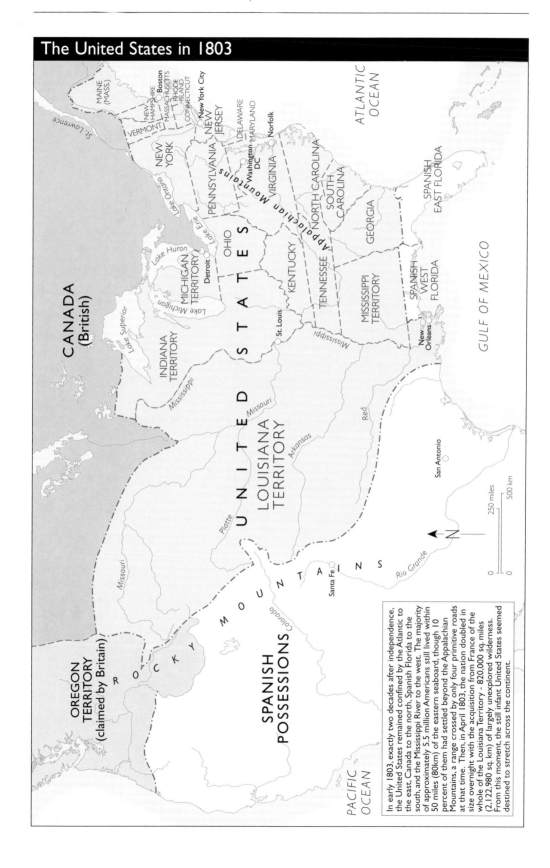

In early 1803, exactly two decades after independence, the United States remained confined by the Atlantic to the east, Canada to the north, Spanish Florida to the south, and the Mississippi River to the west. The majority of approximately 5.5 million Americans still lived within 50 miles (80km) of the eastern seaboard, though 10 percent of them had settled beyond the Appalachian Mountains, a range crossed by only four primitive roads at that time. Then, in April 1803, the nation doubled in size overnight with the acquisition from France of the whole of the Louisiana Territory - 820,000 sq. miles (2,122,980 sq. km) of largely unexplored wilderness. From this moment, the still infant United States seemed destined to stretch across the continent.

The USS *Constitution* in Tripoli harbor, August 3, 1804. On her port quarter American gunboats engage their Tripolitan counterparts. (Mariners' Museum, Newport News, Virginia)

15–20in (38–51cm) thick sides. Notwithstanding her heavy construction, *Constitution* was built in such a streamlined fashion as to enable her to sail at 14 knots (26km/h), faster than any foreign frigate. Her standard armament consisted of 24-pounders (i.e. guns firing 24lb/11kg shot), supplemented by hard-hitting carronades for close-range ship-to-ship encounters. Finally, at 400 officers and men, her crew exceeded that of a typical British frigate by 100 to 150 men.

While the offensive capabilities of the United States were clearly modest by the standards of major contemporary European navies, they could nevertheless make a show of force at the very least, and appeared adequate to the task of bottling up the corsairs in port. Whether, by its presence, an American naval squadron could not only impose a blockade but also inflict serious damage to a heavily fortified port, remained to be seen. For their part, the Barbary States would also have to rely exclusively on their naval forces, paltry though these were, supported by defenses constructed, by bitter paradox, with slave labor.

Extortion on a grand scale

When, on September 3, 1783, Britain recognized the independence of the United States, the new republic had much reason to celebrate. Yet by severing their colonial relationship with the world's greatest naval power, Americans no longer enjoyed the protection afforded them as British subjects and this, in turn, obliged them – if they wished to venture east of Gibraltar – to confront the problem of Barbary piracy on their own. The Mediterranean offered a potentially very lucrative source of income for American ship-owners, so long as they were free from molestation by the Barbary pirates. But as American merchantmen sailed completely unescorted and largely unarmed, with a crew of perhaps a dozen or two at most, it was only a matter of time before the inevitable occurred.

To benefit from the opening of new markets and to pre-empt pirate seizures, in May 1784 Congress instructed the American commissioners in Paris, John Adams, Benjamin Franklin, and Thomas Jefferson, to negotiate commercial treaties with Morocco, Algiers, Tunis, and Tripoli based on principles of equality and reciprocity. Morocco, under Emperor Sidi Muhammad, had already recognized the United States in the spring of 1778 – the first nation to do so – well before independence was a *fait accompli*. Yet the American envoys in Paris, meeting with Moroccan emissaries sent from Tangier to the French capital, reached no agreement. Irritated at America's apparent disinterest in a treaty, the emperor decided to force the United States into action. On October 11, an armed Moroccan vessel out of Salé seized the merchant brig *Betsey*, under Captain James Erwin, while she was en route from Cadiz to Tenerife. Morocco had no desire to engage in war with the United States or enslave its citizens, but demanded a ransom payment and a commercial treaty.

Ignoring calls by some observers to fight rather than endure the national humiliation of paying tribute, Congress, on March 11, 1785, appropriated $80,000 for American diplomats to divide among Morocco and the three other Barbary States. So began America's association with extortion on a grand scale.

This, America's first encounter as an independent nation with Barbary piracy, was to be comparatively benign, for the emperor released the *Betsey*, her crew, and cargo on July 9, 1785, without demanding tribute or other compensation. Thomas Barclay, the commissioner sent to negotiate with Moroccan authorities, concluded a treaty on June 23, 1786, only four days after his arrival at Marrakesh. Morocco would neither exact tribute, nor seize American ships or enslave their crews; both countries would trade on equal terms, with equivalent duties for equivalent goods; and gifts with a value under the $20,000 Barclay had at his disposal were to be provided for the emperor. Thus, at minimal cost, American merchant vessels could pass safely through the Strait of Gibraltar and trade with Morocco. More importantly, the treaty stood as a model upon which the United States could conclude treaties with the other Barbary States based on free trade and no tribute.

But the precedent set with Morocco was not to be repeated. On July 25, 1785, off the Portuguese coast, a 14-gun Algerine xebec seized the schooner *Maria*, en route from Boston to Cadiz and carrying a six-man crew. Within a week another Algerine corsair took the *Dauphin*, out of Philadelphia, with a crew of 15. The circumstances were different from those of Morocco: Algiers, now at war with the United States, was a much more powerful state than its neighbor to the west. Not only had it recently repulsed a major military expedition, but it also obliged Spain to conclude a treaty requiring $2.5 million in presents, tribute, and ransom money. Unlike the emperor of Morocco, the dey of Algiers, the 80-year-old Muhammad V, wished to hold his 21 American captives as slaves, their freedom granted only in exchange for a substantial ransom. The prisoners themselves appealed to their own government for relief, and eventually petitioned Congress as well.

Their efforts were in vain. Prior to the drafting of the Constitution in 1787, the United States had no strong central government capable of directing a coherent, united foreign policy. Under the Articles of Confederation, ratified in March 1781, the nation operated as a confederation of states, each jealous of the other, and none required to provide Congress with tax revenue. With no power of its own to raise funds for the common good of the nation, Congress was severely hampered in its conduct of foreign affairs. The problem was compounded by America's outstanding debt to France, which had provided substantial loans during the Revolution. Thus hamstrung, the American government, faced with Algerine ransom demands which ultimately reached $1 million, found itself incapable of securing its citizens' freedom, whether in the form of funds with which to purchase their release, or in the form of a navy with which to compel the same.

Thus, when the American commissioner, John Lamb, arrived in Algiers on March 25, 1786, the dey approached the negotiations from a position of unassailable strength, expressing himself utterly unwilling to agree to any terms unless they included the payment of a ransom for his American captives. Even when Muhammad drastically reduced his demand to just under $60,000, Lamb declined it, for a ransom payment without a treaty of peace offered no protection against future seizures. Lamb thereupon left Algiers; the slaves remained.

In fact, they would languish in captivity for many years to come. Even after the formal adoption of the Constitution and the establishment of the presidency in 1789,

Congress spent two years engrossed in domestic matters such as trying to tackle the national debt, and though new attempts were made to negotiate with Algiers in 1791, various affairs occupied the attention of the administration of George Washington. When foreign affairs rose to the agenda in 1792, relations with the Barbary States were subordinated by the outbreak of the French Revolutionary Wars, which affected neutral American trade with Europe. Finally, in February 1792 – seven years after the prisoners had been taken – the United States sent Thomas Barclay, who had enjoyed such success in Morocco in 1786, to Algiers, authorized to pay up to $100,000 for peace, $13,500 in annual tribute, and $27,000 in ransom. Muhammad V had died in July 1791, replaced by Ali Hassan, who continued the policy of exacting tribute from numerous European states and knew that the United States possessed neither the means nor the will to stop his corsairs. Barclay's presence achieved nothing; in the course of 1793 the Algerines seized 11 American ships, whose combined crews totalled 104 men. These joined the 15 survivors of the 21 sailors taken in 1785.

These seizures spurred Congress to action. On March 20, 1794, it voted funds for the construction of six frigates costing over a million dollars. President Washington signed it into law seven days later. The dey remained undaunted, and in October he raised his price of peace and ransom to $2 million, making the prospect of release for the prisoners more remote than ever. Negotiations dragged on into 1795, with no progress until, on September 5, the dey reduced his demand to approximately $600,000, or about a third of the original sum required. The American envoy acceded, signed the treaty, and remitted 10 percent of the amount required, promising to pay the balance as soon as he could secure it.

If the treaty with Algiers constituted a humiliation for the United States, the American government believed it had little alternative. The six frigates under construction could not be launched for another two years; in the meantime the

Algerine with musket. Soldiers like this often carried antiquated firearms and highly decorated dirks or swords. (New York Public Library Picture Collection)

captives would go free and American merchants, who stood to bring the nation substantial revenue, would be safe from Algerine pirates.

Circumstances were not as they seemed, however, for the dey now raised his demands, calling for presents valued at more than $200,000 in exchange for the release of his prisoners and the immediate payment of most of the tribute. Some of this was to take the form of naval stores: $21,600 worth of powder, shot, oak planking, masts and, most galling to the Americans, a brig and two schooners. In total, the treaty would actually cost the United States a third more than originally agreed: nearly $1 million according to the Treasury, or about

16 percent of national revenue. This amount, constituting more than any other single expenditure in the federal budget, was well beyond the means of the United States, yet until he received the tribute demanded, the dey would not release his prisoners.

In spite of its inability to meet these terms, Congress ratified the treaty on March 6, 1796, and immediately implemented measures to reduce naval expenditure. The Navy Act of 1794 had contained a clause calling for a halt to shipbuilding in the event of peace with Algiers. The president now translated this into action, though a month later, fearing economic disruption to the shipbuilding community, Congress authorized the completion of three of the six frigates originally ordered: the *United States* and *Constitution*, both of 44 guns, and the 36-gun *Constellation*.

The timing of this reduction could not have been worse, for Algiers was dissatisfied with its treaty, a consequence of the fact that even six months after its signature the dey had still not received his presents and tribute, or the balance of the $600,000 owed to him. On April 3, 1796, he warned that peace and the prisoners' release depended on such payments, though on July 11 he nevertheless released the slaves. In September 1796, the Americans agreed to supply a new 36-gun frigate in exchange for six months' reprieve in submitting the outstanding funds, naval stores, and "gifts." Thus, the United States was not merely providing vast sums of money to Algiers; it was arming Algiers as well.

At last, at the end of 1797, after struggling to raise the outstanding cash and complete the construction of the promised ships, and more than two years after the signature of the treaty, the new administration, now under John Adams, was finally in a position to meet its treaty obligations. In February 1798, Joel Barlow, the American agent at Algiers, handed over the frigate *Crescent* and the schooner *Hamdullah*, much to the dey's satisfaction. The brig *Hassan Bashaw* and the schooner *Skjoldibrand* were still under construction in American shipyards. For Barlow and many of his compatriots, these

deliveries were humiliating, for in addition to tribute the United States was supplying Algiers with the very means of threatening more merchants in the future.

If Algiers appeared satisfied for the moment, its neighbors were not. In 1796, on learning of the treaty between Algiers and the

TOP USS *Constellation* engages the French frigate *Insurgente* in the West Indies on February 9, 1799, during the Quasi-War with France. After taking severe punishment for just over an hour, the French vessel struck her colors. (Mariners' Museum, Newport News, Virginia)

BOTTOM Tripoli in 1803. Contemporary aquatint sketch. (Mariners' Museum, Newport News, Virginia)

Commodore William Bainbridge. Through no fault of his own, this naval officer was obliged to surrender his vessel on two separate occasions. (US Naval Historical Center)

United States, both Tunis and Tripoli threatened war if they did not receive tribute and gifts of similar proportions. Despite his repugnance to the whole distasteful business, Adams chose to placate these extortionists, authorizing Richard O'Brien, the new American agent and himself a former prisoner, to negotiate treaties with the two states.

In the case of Tripoli, the pasha, Yusuf Karamanli, was preparing to unleash his navy and corsairs on the shipping of various countries, and informed resident consuls that their respective governments must conclude treaties of peace and provide the customary "presents" that accompanied such settlements. His threats soon paid dividends: Spain furnished $20,000 and a vessel for the Tripolitan navy; Venice produced $6,000; while even France paid $10,000 and provided two small warships. When states such as Sweden and Denmark refused to comply,

Tripolitan corsairs seized several of their merchantmen and enslaved their crews. Finding this situation intolerable and yet, like the United States, too weak to oppose the pirates, these Scandinavian states eventually paid $5,000 each in annual tribute for the restoration of their ships and men.

It was only a matter of time before American vessels fell victim to Tripolitan piracy; in August corsairs captured the *Sophia* and the *Betsy* (not to be confused with the *Betsey*, seized in 1784), the former being released after she was found to be carrying tribute money for the dey of Algiers. The crew of the *Betsy*, however, were brought ashore and marched off the quayside in chains. O'Brien began negotiations with Tripolitan officials in November 1796, offering $40,000 for peace and the return of the prisoners. As this figure fell well below the massive sum the Americans had already promised to Algiers, the pasha rejected it. When, however, he eventually reduced his demand to the $40,000 originally offered, together with additional cash and naval materiel valued at over $10,000, O'Brien agreed and the treaty was concluded on November 4. The United States now possessed treaties with three of the four Barbary States, with both Algiers and Tripoli receiving annual tribute.

This left Tunis with which to negotiate an agreement. In June 1796, the bey offered a six-month grace period during which he promised that Tunisian corsairs would not harass American vessels. On August 28, 1797, William Eaton agreed to a settlement which – though it did not include annual tribute – still amounted to nearly $180,000 worth of naval stores, including 40 cannon, 12,000 rounds of ammunition, over 3 tons (2.7 tonnes) of gunpowder, and an American-built brig.

Thus, over a decade after the United States had first sought to conclude treaties with all the Barbary States, the task had at last been accomplished, though at a massive price: approximately $1.25 million, or roughly a fifth of the annual federal budget. Such largesse stood as a testament both to America's

President Thomas Jefferson. As early as 1785, while a diplomat in Paris, he opposed the policy of paying tribute to the Barbary powers, and advocated war on the basis that a free and independent nation ought to defend its honor. Fighting would also cost less and earn America respect in Europe. (Public Domain)

weakness and servility, and to its determination, at apparently any cost, to pursue the lucrative trade for which the Mediterranean had been known since antiquity.

The Barbary States were well aware that the United States stood to profit handsomely thanks to its large merchant fleet. Therefore, in violation of its treaty, Algiers demanded two more American-built frigates; notwithstanding public rhetoric to the contrary, Adams agreed. This was not all: in 1799, the United States still owed over $140,000 in tribute to Algiers, quite apart from the three warships already supplied. Tunis and Tripoli, to whom America still owed $150,000, also looked poised to strike while the United States was embroiled in the Quasi-War with France. There seemed, in fact, no end to this catalog of threats and humiliations, including that suffered by Captain William Bainbridge, who arrived at Algiers in the 24-gun frigate *George Washington* in September 1800, bearing tribute in arrears including gunpowder, coffee, and sugar. With his loot ashore, the new dey, Bobba Mustapha, then ordered Bainbridge to convey tribute from the dey to the sultan in

Constantinople aboard the *George Washington*. The mere use of an American warship for such a purpose was not enough: Bainbridge was instructed to fly the Algerine flag in the place of the Stars and Stripes.

Bainbridge might have refused, and indeed contemplated doing so. However, moored as he was beneath the guns of the harbor, aware that the tribute he had brought was over a year and a half in arrears, and concerned that Algiers might resume its seizures of American vessels, he begrudgingly agreed. Reporting this unexpected and degrading episode to the secretary of the navy, Bainbridge bemoaned the powerless state to which his country had been reduced by its failure to confront those who would bully it: "Sir, I cannot help observing that the event of this day makes me ponder on the words INDEPENDENT UNITED STATES." William Eaton expressed in a letter to the secretary of state his disgust that the "first United States ship of war which ever entered the Mediterranean should be pressed into the service of a pirate." Nevertheless, Bainbridge duly sailed for Constantinople on October 19, his ship, in addition to its own crew of over 100, containing a veritable menagerie of cattle, horses, sheep, lions, tigers, antelope, and parrots, not to mention an unwelcome contingent consisting of an Algerine envoy, dozens of his attendants, and a hundred black slaves.

This state of affairs was, however, shortly to change, for during the presidential election campaign of 1800, the Republican contender, Thomas Jefferson, criticized his Federalist opponent, noting how, in spite of a growing Navy, the United States continued to be "subjected to the spoliations of foreign cruisers" and was humiliated by paying "an enormous tribute to the petty tyrant of Algiers." If elected, Jefferson promised to end

A large, three-masted Algerine vessel, capable of propulsion by either sails or oars. By the turn of the 19th century galleys were extremely rare, rendered obsolete by significant improvements over the centuries in gunnery, seamanship, and navigation. (PAF8253; National Maritime Museum, London)

what he condemned as a policy of subservience. Such an undertaking was well-timed, for in July an 18-gun Tripolitan cruiser, the *Tripolino*, captured the brig *Catherine*, bound from New York to Leghorn (now Livorno) and laden with goods worth $50,000. In October 1800, the pasha of Tripoli released the crew, at the same time issuing an ultimatum to the United States: if America did not raise the previously established level of tribute within six months, Tripoli would declare war and attack American merchantmen.

In fact, when on February 26, 1801, the American government refused to comply and Tripoli finally did declare war, it came just weeks before Jefferson, in defiant mood, took office. Writing to James Madison, the secretary of state, the newly elected president declared: "I am an enemy to all these doceurs, tributes and humiliations," continuing, "I know that nothing will stop the eternal increase from

these pirates but the presence of an armed force." This was now at hand, for the undeclared war with France was over, and the United States at last had a small but effective Navy at its disposal. With it Jefferson was prepared to confront the corsairs on the basis that, quite apart from the question of honor, it was more cost-effective to bring an end to tribute through force than to decommission the Navy and remain at the mercy of the Barbary States.

Jefferson reasoned that merely to dispatch a squadron to the Mediterranean might prove sufficient to overawe Tripoli. In any event, America's tributary status had to come to a definite end. To this effect, William Cathcart, the US consul at Tripoli, was instructed to "stifle every pretension or expectation that the United States will on their side make the smallest contribution to him [the pasha] as the price of peace." Morocco remained quiescent; but with both Algiers and Tunis demanding tribute in excess of that stipulated in their existing treaties with the United States – and with Tripoli now actually at war – Jefferson believed he had no choice but to act: force had to be met with force.

To the shores of Tripoli

The First Squadron to the Mediterranean, 1801–02

When the United States sent its first naval force to the Mediterranean in 1801, it had only been independent for less than 20 years and was not prepared for war. Indeed, it had just finished a short-term, undeclared conflict with France involving ship-to-ship encounters in the Atlantic and West Indies. News of Tripoli's new demand, for $25,000 a year in tribute, caused indignation across the country, which was not prepared to concede on top of its payments to the dey of Algiers. In Congress, President Jefferson declared: "It is money thrown away. There is no end to the demands of these powers, nor any security in their promises. The real alternative before us is whether to abandon the Mediterranean or to keep up a cruise on it."

Jefferson had no authorization to declare war without congressional approval, but he consulted his cabinet on May 15. A squadron would be dispatched, though with an uncertain mandate, for Article I, Section 8, of the Constitution invested Congress alone with the power to declare war. The majority view maintained that the squadron should not open offensive operations, though the naval commander was given discretion to engage any Tripolitan vessels that attacked American shipping. He was barred, moreover, from seizing enemy ships or keeping them as prizes. Thus, the restrictions placed on the commander of the squadron were such as to prevent him from taking any initiative: "We enjoin on you the most rigorous moderation, conformity to right & reason, & suppression of all passions, which might lead to the commitment [compromise] of our Peace or our honor."

In May, James Madison, the secretary of state, explained the government's position in a circular letter to all four American consuls in the Barbary States. He also wrote privately on the 20th to William Eaton, the consul at Tunis, observing that the moment was now right for the use of force: "not only is it a provision against an immediate danger, but as we are now at peace and amity with all the rest of the world … the force employed would if at home, be at nearly the same expence [sic], with less advantage to our mariners." In short, the enterprise was economically viable.

Yet American policy remained fatally inconsistent, for even as a squadron was being dispatched to the Mediterranean to confront the Tripolitans, the *George Washington* was en route to Algiers with timber and other stores, as well as partial payment in arrears of $30,000.

On June 2, Commodore Richard Dale, with a small squadron of ships, passed the Virginia Capes, bound for the North African coast. The squadron consisted of the frigates *President* (44 guns), Dale's flagship; the *Philadelphia* (36), commanded by Captain Samuel Barron; the *Essex* (32), under Captain William Bainbridge; and the schooner *Enterprise* (12), commanded by Lieutenant Andrew Sterrett. This modest though respectable force did not, however, include gunboats that could be used to negotiate the shallow waters of Tripoli's rocky coastline or harbor. These were vital if the Americans wished to prevent corsairs from running the blockade that Dale was instructed to impose. Congress estimated the cost of the expedition to reach $500,000, or twice what the pasha demanded in tribute.

A degree of optimism accompanied the expedition, for the senior naval officers aboard the squadron had much to commend them. Commodore Richard Dale had made his name in the Revolutionary War when in

1779, as a young first lieutenant, he led the boarding party from John Paul Jones' *Bonhomme Richard*, from whose rigging he swung from a rope and arrived on the deck of HMS *Serapis* to confront the enemy in hand-to-hand combat. The captain of the *Enterprise*, Andrew Sterrett, was a tough, uncompromising officer, who while a lieutenant aboard the *Constellation* during the recent war with France had in the course of the fighting with the *Insurgente* killed an American sailor who had sought to desert his station. "One fellow," he later told a friend, "I was obliged to run through the body with my sword, and so put an end to a coward."

Owing to poor weather, Dale did not arrive off Tripoli until July 24, at which time he learned of the pasha's declaration of war. The pasha, Dale discovered, was not interested in negotiating: he had declared war because the United States had been delinquent in meeting the terms of the treaty, which the pasha found unfavorable compared to those between America and Algiers and Tunis. In any event, unknown to Dale, the pasha knew that to capitulate would be to imperil his regime, for an unpopular ruler seldom remained long in power in a political culture steeped in conspiracy.

With the diplomatic option closed to him, Dale settled down and established a blockade – such as he could with only four warships – only to discover shortly thereafter that he was running short of fresh water. Sterrett's *Enterprise* was duly detached to Malta, a British possession taken in 1800 after a two-year siege against the French, who had occupied the island in 1798 during Napoleon Bonaparte's expedition to Egypt. On August 1, upon his return from Valetta (now Valletta), Sterrett sighted the 14-gun *Tripoli*, manned by a crew of 80. At the time Sterrett was flying the Union Jack as a means of deceiving potential foes, for Britain and Tripoli were at peace. On hailing the Tripolitan vessel and enquiring after her business and destination, Sterrett was told by the unsuspecting captain that he was seeking out American ships. With this, the Union

Jack swiftly came down, the Stars and Stripes were hoisted in its place, and a volley of American musket fire rang out, to be answered by a weak broadside from the startled Tripolitans.

In his official dispatch to Dale, Sterrett described the action thus:

I have the honor to inform you, that on the 1st of August, I fell in with a Tripolitan ship of war, called the Tripoli, *mounting 14 guns, commanded by Rais Mahomet Rous. An action immediately commenced within pistol shot, which continued three hours incessantly. She then struck her colors. The carnage on board was dreadful; she having 30 men killed and 30 wounded, among the latter was the Captain and first Lieutenant. Her sails, masts and rigging were cut to pieces with 18 shot between wind and water. Shortly after taking possession, her mizzenmast went over the side. Agreeably to your orders, I dismantled her of everything but an old sail and spar. With heartfelt pleasure I add, that the officers and men throughout the vessel* [Enterprise], *behaved in the most spirited and determined manner, obeying every command with promptitude and alertness. We have not had a man wounded, and we have sustained no material damage in our hull or rigging.*

It was an auspicious start for the Americans, but as Sterrett's circumscribed instructions forbade him from taking a prize he was obliged to make the best of circumstances, and cast the enemy's guns overboard and abandoned the ship as a floating wreck.

Back in Washington, Congress, elated by the victory, issued a resolution commending Sterrett, approving funds for a commemorative sword, and granting an extra month's pay to him and his crew. More importantly, the success of the *Enterprise* galvanized public support for the war and enabled Jefferson, in his First Annual Message to Congress, on December 8, 1801, to request further powers for the presidency:

The legislature will doubtless consider whether, by authorizing measures of offense, also, they will place our force on an equal footing with that

of its adversaries. I communicate all material information on this subject, that in the exercise of the important function considered by the Constitution to the legislature exclusively, their judgment may form itself on a knowledge and consideration of every circumstance of weight.

Without technically declaring war, on February 6, 1802, Congress authorized Jefferson to make use of the Navy as he saw fit in order to protect American shipping in the Mediterranean. This removed constitutional restrictions and marked the nation's resolve to use all means necessary to combat Barbary piracy. The legislation authorized naval commanders "to subdue, seize and make prize of all vessels, goods and effects, belonging to the Bey [*sic*] of Tripoli, or to his subjects, and to bring or send the same into port, to be proceeded against, and distributed according to law." This all but stated that the United States was at war, though not obliged to declare it as such. Moreover, since Tripoli had actually declared war on America, the act empowered Jefferson "to cause to be done all such other acts of precaution or hostility as the state of war will justify, and may, in his opinion, require." Thus, the president was free to take offensive action without further recourse to congressional approval. A precedent had been set, by which future presidents could dispatch even substantial armed forces for service abroad without strict adherence to the letter of the Constitution, the most prominent modern example being President Lyndon Johnson's deployment of hundreds of thousands of troops to Vietnam, beginning in 1965.

Meanwhile, Dale, despite his meager force, was preventing corsairs from leaving Tripoli, so rendering safe from attack American merchant vessels sailing into the Mediterranean. On the other hand, without shallow-draught gunboats, the Americans discovered they could not navigate the shallow waters of the coastline or of Tripoli harbor, with the result that three corsairs managed to run the blockade and capture an American merchantman, the *Franklin*, bound

for Marseilles. The captain and eight crewmen were taken to Tripoli, obliging the American consul there to pay $5,000 in ransom for their release. Other corsairs also managed to penetrate Dale's loose blockade, bringing vital supplies of food to the city. Frustrated by the absence of gunboats and alarmed by the imminent expiration of enlistments aboard the *President*, Dale sailed back to Norfolk on April 14, 1802, leaving the other ships of the squadron to continue their vigil off Tripoli. Ambitious to the point of arrogance, Dale soon resigned his commission as a result of a dispute over his desire to become an admiral – a rank that did not yet exist in the Navy and one which Congress declined to create specially for Dale's sake.

The Second Squadron to the Mediterranean, 1802–03

Ideally, command of the Mediterranean squadron, such as it was, ought to have passed to Captain Thomas Truxtun, whose heroic fight with the French frigate *Insurgente* a few years earlier more than recommended him for the post. Yet his desire for status irritated Congress, for he claimed that, as a commodore – and in conformity with the practice of European navies – he was entitled to have a captain aboard his flagship, the *Chesapeake* (38). The Department of the Navy refused to comply, prompting Truxtun to resign his commission, an unfortunate loss to the nation.

Command devolved upon 34-year-old New Yorker Richard Valentine Morris, who had only received his captaincy in 1798. He owed his appointment to political connections through his father, Lewis Morris, a former member of the Continental Congress and a signatory of the Declaration of Independence. Richard Morris' uncle, Gouverneur Morris, had played a prominent role in the Revolution, while his brother, Robert, as a member of the House of Representatives, had helped secure Jefferson's presidential victory over Aaron Burr.

The USS *Enterprise* takes on the corsair *Tripoli* in the first naval encounter of the war, August 1, 1801. (New York Public Library Picture Collection)

This second squadron mounted more guns than the first – 180 instead of 126 – but at $900,000 cost, nearly double that of the first. Morris stepped aboard the *Chesapeake* and sailed from Hampton Roads on April 27, 1802, with five frigates instead of the three led by Dale. From the outset Morris showed poor judgment: with utter disregard for the dangers to be faced, he brought along his wife and young son and joined his squadron without any sense of urgency. When he arrived at Gibraltar on May 31, he wasted his time with social engagements with Royal Navy officers, and did not depart until August 17. Even then he made visits to several Spanish, French, and Italian ports before at last reaching Malta. By the end of the year Morris still had not reached Tripoli; meanwhile, in September, William Eaton wrote to Madison, complaining that he had seen the coast of Tripoli "totally abandoned by our ships of war," since Morris preferred convoying American merchants rather than blockading Tripoli, adding that "our present mode of warfare is not sufficiently energetic." Nor was the American position strengthened by Jefferson's decision in October 1802 to negotiate with Muley Sülcyman, the emperor of Morocco. Refusing to pay the annual tribute, the US government nevertheless authorized its consul in Tangier, James Simpson, to pay as much as $20,000 for peace.

Morris finally weighed from Valetta on January 30, 1803, though a gale obliged him to seek shelter in the harbor. He left again on February 10, but even then made not for Tripoli, but for Tunis, where he wanted to consult with Eaton. Going ashore proved a mistake, for Morris soon found himself taken hostage by the bey. On completing his conference with Eaton and preparing to leave, the commodore had failed to offer the customary formal farewell to the bey, who, affronted, seized him and demanded $34,000 to compensate for the slight. Eaton secured

Morris' release by paying $12,000 of his own money and persuading the Danish consul to stand bond for the remaining $22,000, which Morris sent ashore after arriving back aboard the *Chesapeake*.

The matter closed, Morris, with his wife and son, sailed for Tripoli, where they arrived in late May, more than a year after leaving the United States. In the meantime, the squadron had managed a loose blockade of the port and surrounding coast, with no significant success until early June, when the Americans encountered a flotilla of grain boats in a small bay 35 miles (56km) west of Tripoli. The Americans sailed into the bay and sank them all, destroying 25 tons (23 tonnes) of wheat of which Tripoli was in great need. Believing that he could capitalize on this success, Morris now assumed the guise of a diplomat, and sought to treat for peace with the pasha. Going ashore on June 7 under a flag of truce, the commodore announced his proposals: henceforth the United States would pay Tripoli $5,000 on each occasion in which it sent a new consul, with an additional $10,000 to be paid if the pasha did not seize any American ships for the next five years. The Tripolitans, by now feeling the effects of the blockade and anxious for shipments of imported food, were shocked by such generous terms. Emboldened by the apparent idiocy of the American negotiating position, the pasha then demanded an immediate payment of $200,000 in addition to restitution for the sunken grain boats, plus $200,000 in annual tribute. The talks failed and shortly thereafter Morris, hearing an erroneous report that Tunis and Algiers were massing their ships for war, lifted the blockade of Tripoli and sailed for Malta to concentrate his squadron.

When news of Morris' largesse reached Washington, public and congressional reaction was volcanic. A naval board of inquiry, laying charges of incompetence against him, eventually condemned his conduct in scarcely veiled terms, concluding that Morris "might have acquitted himself well in the command of a single ship, under the orders of a superior, but he was not competent to the command of a squadron." On September 11, therefore, Morris received instructions recalling him from his station; when he arrived in Washington the president stripped him of his commission without so much as a court-martial to hear his defense.

The Third Squadron to the Mediterranean, 1803–04

The third squadron under Commodore Edward Preble consisted of six ships in addition to his own 44-gun *Constitution*: the 36-gun *Philadelphia* (Captain William Bainbridge); the brigs *Argus* (Lieutenant Isaac Hull) and *Siren* (Lieutenant Charles Stewart), both of 16 guns; and three 12-gun schooners, the *Enterprise* (Lieutenant Stephen Decatur), *Nautilus* (Lieutenant Richard Somers), and *Vixen* (Lieutenant John Smith).

Fortunately for the Navy, to command such vessels there was no shortage of competent officers, men who would eventually become known as "Preble's Boys" – a talented cadre of men who would go on to distinguish themselves in the War of 1812. There were five officers in the service senior to the 43-year-old Preble, but Jefferson was determined to place someone with the requisite degree of fighting spirit in Morris' stead. Preble – thin, abrasive, harsh – looked to be the man for the job. He was born in Falmouth (now Portland), Maine, in 1761, the son of Brigadier-General Jedediah Preble, who had fought beside James Wolfe at Quebec in 1759. Though hot-tempered, irascible, and a severe disciplinarian, Edward Preble cared deeply for the welfare of his men, prized loyalty above all other qualities, and was an excellent sailor, having by the time of the Tripolitan War over two decades' service at sea. He took no interest in tending the family farm; the sea was his calling. At age 16, he went to Newburyport, Massachusetts, and signed aboard a privateer. He later became a midshipman on the frigate *Protector* (26 guns), and fought the British 32-gun *Admiral Duff*, and the *Thames*, also a

Commodore Edward Preble, who led the third US squadron dispatched to the Mediterranean. Many of his subordinates would go on to distinguish themselves in independent command during the War of 1812. (Public Domain)

32-gun vessel. When the *Protector* was eventually captured, Preble was sent to rot in the infamous prison hulk *Jersey*, moored off Brooklyn. He endured typhus, malnutrition, and filth for a month before he was exchanged for a British officer through the auspices of a Loyalist who had known his father before the war. He spent the remainder of the war as a lieutenant on the *Winthrop*, a 12-gun vessel, which captured several British privateers off Maine.

After the war, during which his hometown had been destroyed during a British raid, Preble became the first American naval officer to command a vessel east of the Cape of Good Hope. Plagued by chronic stomach ulcers, he eventually tendered his resignation in 1802. The secretary of the navy, Robert Smith, declined to accept it, instead placing Preble on sick leave pending an opening suited to an officer whose

Philadelphia grounded in the shallows of Tripoli harbor. Once she heeled to one side the stricken vessel's guns could not be brought to bear, so attracting enemy gunboats like bees to honey. (US Naval Historical Center)

valuable services the Navy had no wish to lose. Morris' recall in 1803 provided Preble with just such an opportunity.

Preble was fortunate to have the services of competent subordinates. The six-foot tall, heavily-built William Bainbridge, captain of the *Philadelphia*, had, while an 18-year-old first mate aboard a merchantman, personally ended the mutiny of the crew, seizing the ringleader and putting him in irons. In recognition of his services, Bainbridge was promoted to master. He later received a captain's commission in the Navy during the Quasi-War, during which, finding himself completely overwhelmed by the French frigates *Insurgente* and *Volontaire*, he had been forced to surrender his schooner, the *Retaliation*. It was a noble defense, but Bainbridge emerged from the action with the dubious honor of being the first US Navy captain to strike his colors.

Richard Somers, who commanded the 12-gun schooner *Nautilus* under Preble, was not a man to be toyed with. While on shore leave in the Sicilian port of Syracuse with two fellow officers, a group of five brigands confronted him in search of money. Somers parried a sword thrust with his bare hand, and then killed his assailant with the man's sword.

Preble reached Cadiz on September 10, 1803, before passing through the Strait of Gibraltar. There, in thick haze and a moonless night, he made out the figure of a vessel, which he hailed for identification. When the stranger refused to comply, Preble threatened to open fire. An answer, returned by a British officer, declared that he would return fire in that event, stating that he was Sir Richard Strachan, commanding the 84-gun *Donegal*. When summoned to send a boat, Preble refused, instead waiting for one from his opposite. Strachan broke the stand-off by sending a boat himself, and later admitted that his vessel was in fact the considerably smaller 32-gun frigate *Maidstone*. Preble's message had been clear: taking Strachan at his word, the American captain was prepared to fight a vessel mounting nearly twice as many guns as his own. No blood was shed, but Preble's reputation for bravery quickly spread.

Once off Tripoli in September, Preble detached the *Philadelphia* and *Vixen* to maintain the blockade, while the other ships remained further offshore to practice their gunnery. Preble had, in fact, authored his own regulations, the longest section of which covered rules related to gunnery and the boarding of enemy vessels. Like his predecessor, he did not have gunboats at his disposal, but the blockade was to be close, and he issued instructions that all corsairs were to be chased and run down, if possible. If he could not prevent every ship from entering or leaving Tripoli, at least he would challenge them. In any event, Jefferson had learned from previous mistakes, and had asked Congress on February 28 to authorize the purchase or construction of four small warships of 16 or fewer guns, and as many as 15 gunboats. By October these vessels were on their way to join Preble's squadron.

But disaster was about to befall them. On October 31, 1803, while standing off the harbor at Tripoli, lookouts observed two Tripolitan ships attempting to enter the harbor and make for the shore. Bainbridge, in the *Philadelphia*, immediately went in pursuit, but shortly thereafter his frigate ran hard aground on an uncharted reef in 12ft (3.7m) of water. The tide soon forced the vessel to heel radically, rendering her guns useless against the cloud of Tripolitan ships attracted to the scene of the stricken vessel. As the *Philadelphia* lay helpless and with no other course open to him, Bainbridge surrendered the ship and her crew of 307. At high tide the Tripolitans were able to dislodge the prize from the reef and carry her triumphantly into the harbor, there to find a new berth under the guns of the harbor defenses. Triumphant at this unexpected acquisition to his flotilla, the pasha first demanded $1,000 for each captive sailor, raising the total to $450,000, or more than twice what he had required in 1801. Breaking down the figures, he expected to receive $307,000 to ransom the prisoners,

$100,000 for a peace treaty, and $43,000 in presents once the treaty was signed. Apart from this exorbitant demand, the Tripolitans now possessed a heavy frigate that could be refitted and used against the American squadron. To such demands Preble stood defiant, declaring: "I had rather spend the rest of my life in the Mediterranean than consent to either."

Preble was also furious at the loss of the *Philadelphia*. Left with but a single frigate, his own flagship *Constitution*, he wrote to the secretary of the navy:

This affair distresses me beyond description, and very much deranges my plans of operation for the present … Would to God that the Officers and crew of the Philadelphia, *had one and all determined to prefer death to slavery; it is possible such a determination might save them from either.*

He could not have known the impossibility of such a course of action; what he did know, however, was that the ship must be either retaken or destroyed before the Tripolitans could incorporate her into their own navy.

Bainbridge, now a prisoner, was meanwhile thinking the same. From his prison cell in Tripoli, he had via the neutral offices of the Danish consul advised Preble to destroy the vessel. Through an encrypted letter, on December 5 he informed Preble that the Tripolitans had refloated the *Philadelphia* and moored her in 12–14ft (3.7–4.3m) of water. Six or eight boats could with stealth enter the harbor at night and destroy her. The gunboat crews would be on shore, and only a single four-gun battery could oppose an attack. Moreover, elated by their success, the Tripolitans were now less vigilant – and therefore more vulnerable. Bainbridge did not believe the *Philadelphia* could be retaken and sailed to safety: she must therefore be burned.

The plan was exceedingly dangerous, fraught with difficulties of all kinds, and daring beyond measure – but Preble approved it. With such a narrow prospect of success, so perilous a mission could only be carried out by volunteers. The choice of commander to lead the mission was an obvious one: the 25-year-old Stephen Decatur, who had distinguished himself in the Quasi-War. Men eagerly came forward to accompany him aboard the 70-ton (63-tonne) Tripolitan ketch, *Mastico*, which the *Enterprise* had captured and towed to Malta. Decatur appropriately renamed her the *Intrepid*, which he had rigged in the style of a Mediterranean vessel in order to deceive the Tripolitans.

Preble's orders to Decatur, dated January 31, 1804, were direct and succinct:

Sir: You are hereby ordered to take command of the prize ketch Intrepid. *It is my order that you proceed to Tripoli, enter the harbor in the night, board the* Philadelphia, *burn her and make good your retreat. The destruction of the* Philadelphia *is an object of great importance and I rely with confidence on your intrepidity and enterprise to effect it. Lieutenant [Charles] Stewart will support you with the boats of the* Siren *and will cover your retreat with that vessel. On boarding*

the frigate, it is possible you may meet with resistance. It will be well, in order to prevent alarm, to carry all by the sword.

May God prosper you in this enterprise.

Decatur and his crew carefully rehearsed the mission at the Sicilian port of Syracuse, where the men practiced boarding the *Constitution* and setting charges at various points below decks.

The *Intrepid* and *Siren* were off Tripoli on February 7, but just before they entered the harbor a strong northerly gale pushed them back to sea, where they sat for five days awaiting a favorable wind, all the while their provisions dwindling. Finally, on February 16, Decatur, with 75 volunteers and enough combustibles aboard the *Intrepid* to burn the *Philadelphia*, launched the attack. Sailing cautiously through the dark, he intended to

Philadelphia run aground on uncharted rocks. The crew vainly attempted to refloat her, casting overboard guns and equipment from her port side and even cutting away her foremast. (Public Domain)

Boarding the *Philadelphia*, February 16, 1804. Men from the ketch *Intrepid* climb the rigging and over the gunwales, taking the skeleton crew completely by surprise. American morale, both within the squadron and at home, soared in the wake of this remarkable, almost adventure-story, naval exploit. (US Naval Historical Center)

come in under the chains supporting *Philadelphia*'s bowsprit, but he found himself unable to do so owing to the direction of the breeze. Instead, the wind brought *Intrepid* fully under *Philadelphia*'s port side and within sight of the Tripolitan night watch. Decatur had not expected to approach the *Philadephia* unchallenged, and had aboard with him an Arabic-speaking Maltese merchant captain named Salvador Catalano, dressed in Turkish fashion, in case circumstances required communication with the enemy. Hailing the harbor pilot, the interpreter, masquerading as the captain, claimed that he had run the blockade, bearing provisions, but had lost his anchors and required a line with which to fasten himself to the *Philadelphia* for the night. An unsuspecting sentry passed a line, which Decatur's men used to fasten their ketch to the frigate. Moments later the Americans clambered aboard, accompanied by cries of "Philadelphia!"

The Tripolitans raised the alarm, but with surprise in their favor the Americans encountered little resistance. It was clear the enemy had no expectation of an attack in the heart of the harbor and under the guns of the fortress. In fact, many Tripolitans decided to leap overboard rather than fight; others fled below, while those who attempted to repel Decatur's men were quickly overpowered with cutlass and dirk. Once in possession of the ship, the victors fired a flare into the sky, so signaling to the *Siren* that the *Philadelphia* was again in American hands.

Whether Decatur might have sailed the frigate out of the harbor and returned her to active service is now academic; his orders specifically told him to burn the vessel, and that is precisely what he set out to do. Fires were started in various parts of the ship, the flames rapidly spreading into the rigging.

Soon the *Philadephia* was fully ablaze, her loaded guns discharging as the fiercely glowing ship, her cable burnt through, began to drift aimlessly. Meanwhile, *Siren*'s boats had attached hooks to the *Intrepid* and were towing her and all of Decatur's men, only one of whom sustained an injury, to safety. As *Philadephia* passed just under the pasha's castle, the fire finally reached her magazine, and in an enormous, deafening explosion – heard by tens of thousands of people for miles around, shaking houses across Tripoli, and propelling wreckage high into the air – the once proud frigate was no more.

Back in America, news of the exploit electrified the nation, where the public rejoiced with fulsome expressions of national pride. For what Vice-Admiral Horatio Nelson, victor of the battles of the Nile and Copenhagen (and, the following year, Trafalgar), reputedly called "the most bold and daring act of the age," Congress voted Decatur a sword and made him a captain over the heads of seven other officers awaiting promotion, making the hero of the hour the youngest officer in the US Navy ever to hold that rank. The destruction of the *Philadelphia* could not fail to elicit a response from the pasha, who from his castle heard the explosion and saw its aftermath. In anticipation of an immediate full-scale American attack, Yusuf ordered the prisoners to be kept under close guard. Within days, the pasha dropped his claim for millions of dollars, and eventually offered to make a truce, with no payments for five years. Elsewhere, the American consul in Tunis, George Davis, observed that his compatriots' exploit "has made much noise in Tunis, and is the only occasion on which I have heard our Countrymen spoken of with due respect." Force, it seemed, was beginning to make itself felt.

Preble did not remain idle. Determined to capitalize on his success, he approached the government of the Kingdom of Naples, requesting the loan or hire of a few gunboats and mortar boats with which to bombard Tripoli. The king obliged, and on August 3, three months after his blockade of Tripoli

Decatur's raid on the *Philadelphia*, February 16, 1804

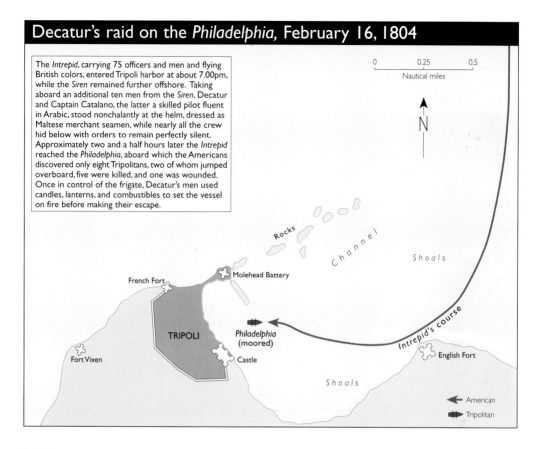

The *Intrepid*, carrying 75 officers and men and flying British colors, entered Tripoli harbor at about 7.00pm, while the *Siren* remained further offshore. Taking aboard an additional ten men from the *Siren*, Decatur and Captain Catalano, the latter a skilled pilot fluent in Arabic, stood nonchalantly at the helm, dressed as Maltese merchant seamen, while nearly all the crew hid below with orders to remain perfectly silent. Approximately two and a half hours later the *Intrepid* reached the *Philadelphia*, aboard which the Americans discovered only eight Tripolitans, two of whom jumped overboard, five were killed, and one was wounded. Once in control of the frigate, Decatur's men used candles, lanterns, and combustibles to set the vessel on fire before making their escape.

had begun, Preble opened a series of attacks intended to destroy the Tripolitan fleet and the pasha's shore defenses so as to compel the release of the Americans held captive in the city. With small craft from Naples finally at his disposal, Preble sent Decatur with six gunboats and two bomb ketches deep into the harbor. The bomb vessels, mounting heavy mortars for high-trajectory shore bombardment, began to lob shells into the city, while the gunboats – highly maneuverable but armed with only one or two cannon – gradually made their way toward the Tripolitans, who had 19 gunboats, a brig, two schooners, and a galley.

Circumstances favored the Tripolitans even more when an unexpected shift in the direction of the wind prevented three of the American gunboats from entering the harbor. Those inside included Gunboat No. 4, led by Stephen Decatur; Gunboat No. 2, commanded by his younger brother, Lieutenant James Decatur; and Gunboat

No. 6, led by Sailing Master John Trippe. Undaunted by the absence of their three consorts, these commanders continued on their course towards the Tripolitan flotilla. The American tactics were straightforward and effective: approach to within pistol-shot range, fire canister shot onto the enemy's deck, and, before the Tripolitans could regain their senses, close, board, and take the opposing vessel with cutlass, pike, and pistol. Stephen Decatur's gunboat did just that, quickly seizing one of its counterparts.

While the gunboats were busy engaging each other, Preble took the *Constitution* into the harbor and began to bombard the shore batteries at close range. Preble was nearly killed when a 32lb (14.5kg) shot entered an open gun port, narrowly missed him, crashed into a cannon, and burst into fragments, wounding a marine. Having silenced the shore batteries, the *Constitution* proceeded to sink several Tripolitan merchantmen and fire several dozen rounds into the pasha's castle

and the town itself. The sight of the *Constitution* unleashing her broadsides in the harbor brought cheer to the American prisoners in Tripoli, and Bainbridge witnessed the whole scene. He later wrote:

The *Philadelphia* blazing furiously as the *Intrepid* makes her escape. While still impressive in reality, the height of the fortifications depicted in this 19th-century print is slightly exaggerated. (Library of Congress Prints and Photographs Division)

At the commencement of the bombardment, the Pasha surveyed the squadron from his palace windows, and affected to ridicule any attempt which might be made to injure either the batteries or the city. He promised the spectators on the terraces that rare sport would present be enjoyed by observing the triumph of his boats over the Americans. In a few minutes, however, he became convinced of his error, and precipitately retreated with an [sic] humble and aching heart to his bomb-proof chamber.

American success appeared complete until, as the gunboats began to withdraw from the harbor, Decatur learned of his brother's death. James Decatur had forced a Tripolitan gunboat to surrender, but as he had jumped aboard to claim his prize, the enemy captain, brandishing a pistol, had shot him in the head. He had fallen back into his own boat, and in the confusion the enemy had made their escape. Trippe dropped back and brought the dreadful news to Stephen Decatur, who, enraged, promptly steered for the gunboat that he thought was responsible for his brother's death, seeking revenge. It is not clear if in fact he caught up with the gunboat actually responsible, but Decatur and 11 other sailors leapt the rails and boarded the enemy vessel nonetheless.

Alexander MacKenzie, a participant in the action who wrote an account of it for Preble, described the Tripolitan captain as "gigantic," and brandishing a "heavily ironed boarding pike." With this he challenged Decatur, but in parrying the thrust the American broke his cutlass at the hilt. The captain made another thrust, piercing Decatur's arm and cutting into his chest. Decatur, "tearing the weapon from the wound," took hold of his assailant, and as the two men grappled on the deck, another Tripolitan swung his sword at Decatur's head from behind. A severely wounded American sailor named Reuben James, whose injuries prevented the use of his arms, interposed his body and took the blow himself on his head. As Decatur and the Tripolitan captain struggled on the deck, Decatur pulled a pistol from his belt, thrust it

against the back of his antagonist, and pulled the trigger. As MacKenzie later described the scene, "Decatur, disengaging himself from the heap of wounded and slain, which the struggle had gathered around him, stood again that day a victor on the enemy's deck."

With their captain dead, the Tripolitan crew promptly surrendered, and the remaining gunboats now fled for safety deeper into the harbor. By the end of the action, three Tripolitan gunboats had been captured, one had been sunk, and the remaining 15 had suffered substantial damage. Fifty-two Tripolitans had been killed and 56 taken prisoner.

Despite the destruction wrought by Preble's squadron, the pasha refused to release his captives. Bad weather obliged Preble to call off his attack, but he returned on August 7 and 25, and again on

Destruction of the *Philadelphia*. The *Intrepid* makes her escape in the confusion, while a Tripolitan battery positioned in a castellated tower fires in vain. (US Naval Historical Center)

Bombardment of Tripoli, August 3, 1804. Preble's squadron exchanges fire with corsairs and land-based artillery, while in the background trails of smoke show the course of mortar fire descending on the city in a high-angle arc. (Library of Congress Prints and Photographs Division)

September 3, on all occasions pounding the city and its defenses and engaging enemy vessels in the harbor. However, the attacks were less successful than the Americans expected. The Tripolitan minister of foreign affairs, Sidi Muhammed Dghies, told the French chargé d'affaires that "since the Effusion of blood had already commenced, his country was bent upon continuing the war." Peace, the Tripolitan minister declared, remained impossible for less than two or three hundred thousand dollars. The city had received some damage, but not substantial.

Aware that the situation had not materially improved, concerned that reinforcements from home under Commodore Samuel Barron had not yet arrived, and anxious about the worsening weather, Preble decided on one final attack. On September 4, the ketch *Intrepid*, which Decatur had used in his operation to burn the *Philadelphia*, was converted into an explosion vessel, with 15,000lb (8,818kg) of gunpowder filling her hold and 250 13in fused shells piled on her decks. This floating bomb was to be brought alongside the walls of the castle, in the midst of the enemy's ships, and detonated; the crew were to make their escape in the *Constitution*'s gig. Volunteers came forward in droves to offer their services for the operation, though few were actually required. In the end the mission was to be carried out by Master Commandant Richard Somers, Lieutenant Joseph Israel, and Midshipman Henry Wadsworth, together with four sailors from the *Nautilus* and six from the *Constitution*.

At 9.00pm, with a weak breeze, the *Intrepid* glided slowly into the harbor, low-lying fog obscuring the view of the observers who lay further offshore. Suddenly, an alarm gun from the Tripolitan position rang out, and moments later the shore batteries began a heavy fire. In a blinding flash the *Intrepid* disintegrated in a thunderous explosion, and a sheet of flame, mingled with debris, shot up into the air, accompanied by trails of light left by the

FOLLOWING PAGE Lieutenant Stephen Decatur in mortal combat aboard a Tripolitan gunboat. Quarter Gunner Reuben James, though disabled, selflessly protects Decatur from almost certain death. (US Naval Historical Center)

bursting shells. According to a sailor aboard the *Constitution*, "the flash illuminated the whole heavens around, while the terrific concussion shook everything far and near." The crew of the *Intrepid* was instantly killed in the inferno, and though it is not clear precisely what had happened, it appears the ship had exploded prematurely when a Tripolitan shot had set off the arsenal of shot aboard *Intrepid*. In any event, the ketch had blown up several hundred yards short of her target, and thus had caused no damage either to the fortifications or the enemy vessels in the harbor. When disfigured bodies of 12 of the 13 crewmen were later washed ashore, the pasha forced Bainbridge to see them. Preble, meanwhile, conscious that the changing weather would soon render further operations difficult and concerned by his ships' severe shortage of ammunition and water, maintained his blockade and waited impatiently for the arrival of Barron's squadron.

The Fourth Squadron to the Mediterranean, 1804–05

Five days after the loss of the *Intrepid*, reinforcements arrived off Tripoli, including the frigates *President*, *Congress*, *Constellation*, and *Essex*, so marking the end of Preble's distinguished tenure as commander of the Mediterranean squadron. This, the fourth squadron sent out since hostilities had begun in 1801, now brought the total American force to six frigates (out of 13 available to the Navy), six smaller ships including brigs and schooners, two bomb vessels, and ten gunboats, at a cost of $1.5 million, three times that of the first squadron. Flying his flag aboard the *President* was Commodore Samuel Barron, who held seniority over Preble. The secretary of the navy had assumed that Preble would be prepared to remain on station as second-in-command. Preble's sense of pride rendered this impossible, and he decided to return to the United States, though not before

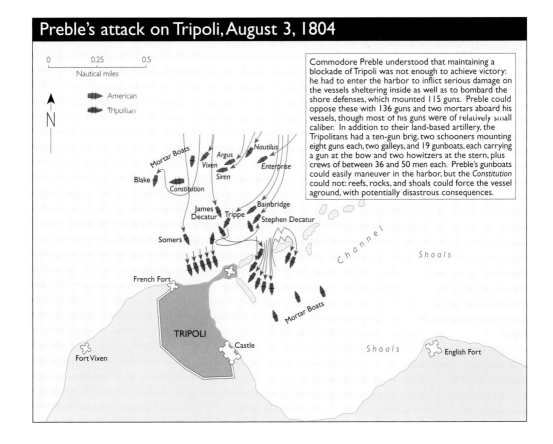

Preble's attack on Tripoli, August 3, 1804

0   0.25   0.5

Nautical miles

N

American
Tripolitan

Mortar Boats
Argus
Nautilus
Vixen
Enterprise
Blake
Siren
Constitution
James Decatur
Trippe
Bainbridge
Stephen Decatur
Somers
French Fort
TRIPOLI
Castle
Fort Vixen
Channel
Shoals
Mortar Boats
Shoals
English Fort

Commodore Preble understood that maintaining a blockade of Tripoli was not enough to achieve victory: he had to enter the harbor to inflict serious damage on the vessels sheltering inside as well as to bombard the shore defenses, which mounted 115 guns. Preble could oppose these with 136 guns and two mortars aboard his vessels, though most of his guns were of relatively small caliber. In addition to their land-based artillery, the Tripolitans had a ten-gun brig, two schooners mounting eight guns each, two galleys, and 19 gunboats, each carrying a gun at the bow and two howitzers at the stern, plus crews of between 36 and 50 men each. Preble's gunboats could easily maneuver in the harbor, but the *Constitution* could not: reefs, rocks, and shoals could force the vessel aground, with potentially disastrous consequences.

his officers presented him with a signed scroll containing words of thanks and admiration. Sailing via Valetta, Syracuse, and Naples, the commodore was welcomed at each place by the salute of cannon and the cheers of foreign sailors hanging from the yards and rigging of their ships. When, on March 4, 1805, Preble reached Washington, Congress voted him a sword and a gold medal, while politicians delivered a series of speeches expressing the nation's gratitude for his services.

Outside Tripoli, Barron had brought more than reinforcements; he had instructions to conduct an ambitious joint land-sea operation, whose origins dated back to November 1803, when the pasha's brother, Hamet, had written to President Jefferson, proposing an expedition against Tripoli with American assistance. Hamet explained that some years before, his father Ali Karamanli had assigned Hassan, the eldest of his three sons, to be his successor. Yusuf, the third son, murdered Hassan, thus making Hamet, by the laws of primogeniture, heir to the throne. Yusuf then forced Hamet to take refuge in

Desperate struggle on the decks of a Tripolitan gunboat. A pirate prepares to deliver the coup de grâce *to the prostrate Decatur, who saves himself with a pistol drawn from his belt, as the gallant James lies severely wounded at his feet. (Library of Congress Prints and Photographs Division)*

Tunis, and though Hamet was later allowed to control Derna (alternatively Derne) – a minor port in the eastern part of the country – he was eventually driven off by troops sent by Yusuf, who for safe-keeping held Hamet's wife and five children hostage to prevent Hamet from staging a coup. Hamet, therefore, proposed to the American government that he would assemble an Arab force, capture Derna, and then move on Tripoli itself. If Jefferson agreed to support this venture, Hamet promised to re-establish peace between their two nations. For the sake of $40,000 and the necessary military supplies, Hamet argued, the United States could have peace and an end to tributary payments.

Accompanying Barron's squadron was William Eaton, a former captain in the Army and consul at Tunis, now designated an

The *Intrepid* explodes before reaching her target. Contemporary opinion held that the crew, anxious that the ketch not fall into the hands of approaching Tripolitan vessels, deliberately blew her up. A direct hit from an enemy round shot nevertheless remains the more plausible explanation for the explosion. (US Naval Historical Center)

"agent for the Navy." He came with authorization from Jefferson to assist Hamet with arms, ammunition, and funds with which to overthrow Yusuf and establish Hamet as pasha – a position, in any event, to which Hamet appeared to have a legitimate claim. At the same time, Tobias Lear, the US consul at Tripoli, was to use his extensive discretionary powers to negotiate a treaty of peace with Yusuf. Barron was to continue the blockade of the enemy capital and to cooperate with Eaton "in all such measures as may be deemed the best calculated to effectuate a termination" of the war.

Jefferson knew he was taking an unprecedented step: there was no concealing the fact that this plan constituted direct intervention in the internal affairs of a foreign power. Madison, the secretary of state, wrote to Eaton to justify this extraordinary course of action:

Although it does not accord with the general sentiments or views of the United States, to intermeddle in the domestic contests of other countries, it cannot be unfair, in the prosecution of a just war, or the accomplishment of a reasonable peace, to turn to their advantage, the enmity and pretensions of others against a common foe.

This was all the more extraordinary in light of the fact that, technically speaking, the United States was not at war with Tripoli, as Congress had never officially declared it. Thus the conflict set two important precedents in American foreign policy: the president's right to engage in hostilities without a declaration of war; and the right, based on the president's own definition of a "just war," to subvert a foreign government – what has recently become known as "regime change."

North African soldiers. Eaton's troops encountered
soldiers such as these during their advance on Derna.
(New York Public Library Picture Collection)

Accordingly, Eaton sailed to the Egyptian
coastal city of Alexandria aboard the brig
Argus (Captain Isaac Hull), where he
arranged to meet Hamet, then recruiting
men for his expedition. The two men signed
an agreement on February 23, 1805, by
which Eaton promised American support
in the form of provisions, money, and
ammunition, and to establish Hamet as
pasha of Tripoli. Once in power, Hamet was
to reimburse the United States for the cost of
the operations by transferring to it all the
tribute paid to Tripoli by Sweden, Denmark,
and the Batavian Republic (Holland). Eaton
would hold senior command of the
expeditionary force, a motley combination
of Hamet's Egyptian mercenaries, the
handful of Tripolitans loyal to Hamet's cause,

eight US Marines, and one US Navy
midshipman. This bizarre polyglot force of
uncertain effectiveness numbered about
500 men.

The expedition left Alexandria on March 8,
bound for Derna, on an immensely long
500-mile (805km) march across the Libyan
Desert. At the same time, Hull was to sail to
a point on the coast close to Derna where he
could land supplies and reinforcements upon
Eaton's arrival. Progress by land started well
enough, but when on April 8 food ran low
and starvation loomed, Hamet and many of
his followers staged a revolt against Eaton,
with the intention of abandoning the
expedition and marching back to Egypt.
When Eaton posted the marines and other
soldiers to guard the supply tent, 200 Arab
horsemen charged them, at the last moment
wheeling about and returning their scimitars
to their sheathes. Amazingly, the marines
kept their heads and held their fire. A full-

The March to Derna, March–April 1805

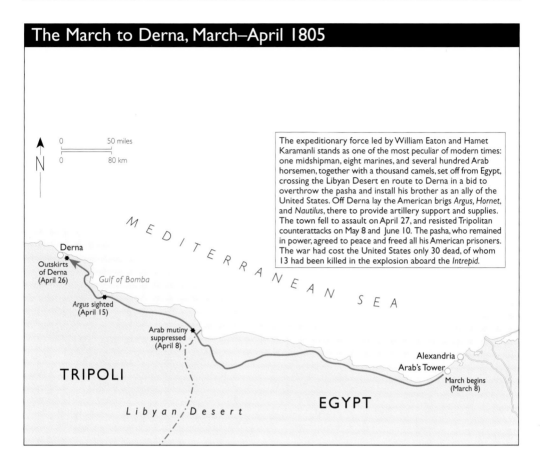

0   50 miles
0   80 km

N

MEDITERRANEAN SEA

Derna

Outskirts
of Derna
(April 26)

Gulf of Bomba

Argus sighted
(April 15)

Arab mutiny
suppressed
(April 8)

TRIPOLI

Libyan Desert

Alexandria
Arab's Tower

March begins
(March 8)

EGYPT

The expeditionary force led by William Eaton and Hamet Karamanli stands as one of the most peculiar of modern times: one midshipman, eight marines, and several hundred Arab horsemen, together with a thousand camels, set off from Egypt, crossing the Libyan Desert en route to Derna in a bid to overthrow the pasha and install his brother as an ally of the United States. Off Derna lay the American brigs *Argus*, *Hornet*, and *Nautilus*, there to provide artillery support and supplies. The town fell to assault on April 27, and resisted Tripolitan counterattacks on May 8 and June 10. The pasha, who remained in power, agreed to peace and freed all his American prisoners. The war had cost the United States only 30 dead, of whom 13 had been killed in the explosion aboard the *Intrepid*.

scale mutiny was thus averted, and Eaton, fluent in Arabic, managed to persuade the men to continue with the arduous journey. After great exertion, and six weeks' marching, the mixed force – more a rabble than a military force – finally reached the outskirts of Derna on April 25.

Derna was lightly defended, for the garrison of 800 men was confident that the American ships could not negotiate the port's shallow waters and bring their guns within effective range of the fortification and its dozen cannon. A landward assault was anticipated, but the force dispatched by the pasha to aid the town was still a few days' march away to the west. In this respect the defenders badly miscalculated, for their opponents' ingenuity and boldness in making the arduous overland journey exceeded their expectations. While Eaton wrote a conciliatory letter on the 26th, seeking the garrison's capitulation in the name of Hamet, the town's governor was in no mood to oblige, returning the ominous answer, "My head or yours."

After landing their cargoes of weapons and ammunition for Eaton on the 28th, the *Argus*, *Hornet*, and the *Nautilus* were light enough to make their way into the harbor, and once within range of the outer fort they began to fire on it. The defenders returned fire for about an hour before abandoning their guns in the face of superior firepower and withdrawing into the town. Then, at about 3.00pm, Lieutenant Presley O'Bannon, at the head of his party of marines and midshipmen, stormed the fort from the beach, while Hamet's men attacked from the landward side. O'Bannon lowered the Tripolitan flag and planted the Stars and Stripes on the walls of the fort, the first such feat for American forces on foreign soil. Caught between both forces, the Tripolitans surrendered at about

Captain James Barron. Brother of Commodore Samuel Barron, commander of the fourth squadron dispatched to the Mediterranean, he commanded the 32-gun frigate *Essex*. He had served as Bainbridge's second during the latter's duel in 1801. (US Naval Historical Center)

William Eaton. While serving as the American consul at Tunis in 1801, he urged war against Tripoli: "If the United States will have a free commerce in this sea they must defend it." Four years later he led an unlikely force consisting of a handful of American sailors and marines, and several hundred Arab mercenaries and adventurers. (Mariners' Museum, Newport News, Virginia)

4.00pm, leaving Eaton and Hamet's men in possession of the town and fort, all at a cost of one marine killed and two others wounded, together with ten of Hamet's men. Eaton himself had been wounded by a musket ball through his left wrist.

Flushed with victory, Eaton now planned to move on Tripoli itself, another 400 miles (644km) to the west. He was determined to retain hold of Derna and see the war to a successful end, with Hamet installed as pasha. He was particularly anxious lest the United States enter into premature negotiations for peace while the initiative remained in its hands. In this Eaton was to be disappointed, for he learned that on June 4 Lear had concluded a treaty with Tripoli. By its terms, Derna was to be immediately evacuated. Eaton conceded that the treaty was "more favorable – and, separately

considered, more honorable than any peace obtained by any Christian nation with a Barbary regency at any period within a hundred years," but he was anxious that his country not abandon Hamet and his forces to an uncertain fate with Yusuf still in power.

Lear explained the course of his negotiations. He had rejected out of hand the pasha's demand for $200,000 in exchange for peace and the ransoming of the prisoners, as well as the return of all Tripolitan prisoners and property currently in American hands. He had, however, made a

RIGHT Marine First Lieutenant Presley O'Bannon, the 21-year-old Virginian who in the spring of 1805 led the small party of US Marines and midshipmen which marched across the Libyan Desert to reach the Tripolitan port town of Derna. (Public Domain)

counteroffer: $60,000 for ransom, but nothing explicitly for peace. Lear rightly believed that the capture of Derna had certainly strengthened his hand in the negotiations, as had the blockade, which was beginning to cause food shortages and growing unrest amongst the populace. Yusuf, for his part, probably concluded that if a scratch force could take Derna, a larger force could seize Tripoli itself. In truth, the full extent of Eaton's influence on the outcome of the talks in Tripoli is not known, but in any event Yusuf accepted Lear's terms: the United States would return Derna, and Hamet was to leave Tripolitan territory, after which his family would be restored to him. The Americans would pay $60,000 for the release of Captain Bainbridge, the crew of the *Philadelphia*, and all other American prisoners in Tripolitan hands. Finally, the pasha promised to cease his attacks on American shipping.

But although peace was at last re-established between Tripoli and the United States, it was not to spell the end of America's problems with the remaining Barbary States.

Commodore Stephen Decatur, United States Navy

One of America's greatest naval heroes, Stephen Decatur was born in Sinepuxent, Maryland, on January 5, 1799, to a prominent naval family. Commissioned as a midshipman aboard the 44-gun *United States* on April 30, 1798, the very day the Department of the Navy was established, he served in the Quasi-War against France and rose rapidly to lieutenant, receiving his commission on May 21, 1799. Decatur is best associated with his role in the war against Tripoli, where he initially commanded the 12-gun schooner *Enterprise*, with which he captured the Tripolitan ketch *Mastico* on December 23, 1803. With this prize, renamed *Intrepid*, he daringly led a raid into Tripoli harbor on the night of February 16, 1804, boarding the former American frigate *Philadelphia*, and setting her on fire with combustibles without the loss of a single man.

The event has served as an inspiration to US Navy personnel ever since. One naval officer, writing in 1942, said of the event: "To the example of personal gallantry thus set by Decatur before Tripoli, and the chivalrous spirit communicated to his companions in arms, we may ascribe in no small degree the heroic tone which has characterized all the after achievements of our navy." The deed made him an instant national hero and earned for him a captaincy, making him, at the age of 25, the youngest officer of that rank in the history of the United States Navy. He displayed considerable intrepidity yet again when, during the gunboat action in Tripoli harbor on August 3, he and his men boarded and captured an enemy gunboat, and avenged the death of his brother, James, by seizing another. His life was saved by Quarter Gunner Reuben James, who, though himself badly wounded in both arms, placed himself between Decatur and an assailant poised to deliver a blow to the back of Decatur's head with a scimitar. Decatur wrote to a fellow officer on January 9, 1805, saying of the affair: "I find hand to hand is not child's play, 'tis kill or be killed."

After the war with Tripoli, Decatur oversaw the construction of gunboats at Rhode Island and in Virginia, and took command of the frigate *Chesapeake* in June 1807. During the War of 1812, he commanded the frigate *United States*, aboard which, in a bitterly fought action on October 25, 1812, he captured HMS *Macedonian*. In May 1814 he was assigned to the *President* and in July commanded naval forces at New York. Owing to the blockade of the Atlantic coast by the Royal Navy, Decatur was forced to remain in port for many months, but he managed to

Stephen Decatur, hero of the Tripolitan War, whom a fellow officer described as having a "peculiarity of manner and appearance calculated to engross the attention – the form and look of a hero." (US Naval Historical Center)

The frigate *Philadelphia* burning in Tripoli harbor. In an age replete with stirring examples of derring-do, Decatur's achievements rank high on the list. (US Naval Historical Center)

put to sea in January 1815. Pursued by a numerically superior British squadron on the 15th, Decatur took a battering and failed to shake off his pursuers. Despite a spirited resistance, he eventually accepted the inevitable, as he explained to the secretary of the navy: "Then situated, with about one fifth of my crew killed and wounded, my ship crippled, and a more than fourfold force opposed to me, without a chance of escape left, I deemed it my duty to surrender."

No sooner had the war with Britain come to an end than Decatur was dispatched in command of a squadron for the Mediterranean, where he dictated peace terms to Algiers, Tunis, and Tripoli, so putting a definitive end to Barbary raids on American shipping. From December 20, 1815, he served as a member of the Board of Navy Commissioners, in which capacity he opposed giving Captain James Barron

command of a ship of the line. This resulted in a duel, held at Bladensburg, Maryland, and fought at only eight paces, on March 22, 1820. Both men were wounded in the contest, Decatur mortally. The whole nation mourned his death.

That Decatur was brave there can be no doubt. Apart from his exploits in combat, while aboard the first ship under his command, the *United States*, Decatur had challenged to a duel the mate of a merchantman who had refused to return deserters from Decatur's ship. Decatur wounded his opponent in the hip, with no injury to himself. In another incident, in July 1801 as first lieutenant aboard the *Essex*, he wrote an angry message to the commander of a Spanish guard ship that had fired over one of his ship's shore boats. When Decatur declared that he would come aboard the following morning in search of an explanation, the Spanish officer did not risk being present, prompting Decatur to leave a threatening message: "Lieutenant Decatur pronounces him a cowardly scoundrel and that, when they meet on

TOP *Intrepid*, illuminated by moonlight, entering Tripoli harbor. (US Naval Historical Center)

BOTTOM Decatur finishes off his assailant with the timely use of his pistol during the gunboat action of August 3, 1804. (US Naval Historical Center)

shore, he will cut his ears off." No such encounter ever took place, but the Spanish thereafter ceased to annoy American vessels.

Decatur had also served as a second in a duel on February 14, 1803, between 16-year-old Midshipman Joseph Bainbridge (younger brother of William Bainbridge), of the USS *New York*, and James Cochran, secretary to the British governor of Malta, Sir Alexander Ball. After becoming the object of insulting remarks about the US Navy from a group of British officers attending an opera in Valetta, the midshipman knocked down his tormenter. Decatur, as the second, established the rules: to compensate for the fact that Bainbridge's adversary was a crack shot known to have killed several men in previous duels, Decatur declared that the duelists exchange fire at four, rather than the customary ten, paces, thus leaving no possibility of missing. "Good Lord, sir," replied his opposite number, "that looks like murder." "Not murder," Decatur replied, "but surely death." Thus was the result – with Bainbridge the survivor.

Apart from his naval exploits and dueling prowess, Decatur is remembered for the patriotic toast he made in April 1816: "Our Country! In her intercourse with foreign nations may she always be in the right; but our country, right or wrong." Energetic and sociable, he was known to possess a strong sense of honor. In his mid-19th century biography of Decatur, Alexander Slidell Mackenzie observed that he:

… possessed, in an eminent degree, the happy art of governing sailors rather by their affections than their fears. He was averse to punishment, and rarely had occasion to resort to it, being usually able to rely, for the preservation of discipline, on the reluctance of his inferiors to displease him. It was remarked of him … by an officer, that "he seemed, as if by magic, to hold a boundless sway over the hearts of seamen at first sight." Such a conquest could only have been gained by a just regard for their rights, a watchful care of their comfort, and a sympathy in their feelings.

Stephen Decatur, the US Navy's answer to Horatio Nelson. Decatur's fearlessness and determination did more than propel him to fame; they helped establish the high standard for conduct that would stand the young navy in good stead a decade later in the conflict with Britain. (US Naval Historical Center)

Lewis and Clark explore the American West, 1804–06

The expedition undertaken by Meriwether Lewis and William Clark stands as a monument to endurance and the American spirit of adventure. The expedition – contemporaneous with the war against Tripoli and inspired by the same president, Thomas Jefferson, who first sent warships to the Mediterranean – ventured quite literally into the unknown. It was to conduct important studies of the wildlife, terrain, and Native American peoples of the Louisiana Territory and beyond, as far as the Pacific, as well as, most importantly, to map the course of the epic journey. Precisely at the time that Eaton and his marines were struggling across the sands of the Libyan Desert in searing heat, thousands of miles away Lewis and Clark, with their small party of intrepid explorers, were moving west in dugout canoes up the treacherous white waters of the Missouri River, in modern-day North Dakota, witnesses to an extraordinary landscape hitherto unseen by white men. These two seemingly unconnected events in fact shared an unmistakeable, crucial feature: only a generation after independence, the United States, brimming with unquenchable energy, was rapidly expanding west across North America even as it was simultaneously extending its military might east, thousands of miles from its shores. This was more than mere symbolism: the nation was extending its reach – its physical boundaries at home, and its power abroad.

In 1801, the American frontier stood only as far west as the Mississippi, with the vast majority of the Americans living on or close to the Atlantic seaboard. After Congress agreed to fund the expedition in January 1803, Meriwether Lewis, Jefferson's personal secretary, began something of a crash course in zoology, botany, medicine, and celestial navigation, thus acquiring all the skills necessary for survival and the study of the territories through which he would pass. Lewis would share command with William Clark, the two men having served together in the Army. Before the expedition began, in the summer of 1803 the United States acquired the Louisiana Territory: 820,000 sq. miles (2,122,980 sq. km) for $15 million, or 3 cents an acre. Overnight, America had doubled in size, but nothing was known of these vast new lands.

The two men gathered supplies and a 55ft (16.8m) keelboat and established a base at Camp Wood, on the east bank of the Mississippi, upstream from St. Louis. Having recruited about 50 men with various skills, the expedition, known as the Corps of Discovery, set out on May 14, 1804, up the Missouri River. Before the end of the month they had passed beyond the last white settlement on the river. Their first contact with western Native Americans took place in early August somewhere north of present-day Omaha. The expedition demonstrated the various forms of technology taken with them, including compasses, telescopes, magnets, and firearms.

In late August, after one of the expedition's members had died, possibly from appendicitis, near present-day Sioux City, Iowa, Lewis and Clark met with leaders of the Yankton Sioux in present-day South Dakota. They then tirelessly pressed on, reaching the Great Plains, where they encountered wildlife not known in the east, including antelope, various species of deer, and coyotes. Their first encounter with trouble took place in late September, near present-day Pierre, South Dakota, when the Lakota refused to let the expedition proceed upriver unless it surrendered one of its boats, though fortunately a Native American chief managed to settle the matter without a fight.

By late October the expedition reached the area around what is now Bismarck, North Dakota, the site of Mandan and Hidatsa villages. There the expedition employed as an interpreter a French Canadian fur trader living with the Native Americans, together with his wife, a Shoshone named Sacagawea. With temperatures dropping well below freezing, the expedition camped for the winter at Fort Mandan, which the men constructed across the river from the main Mandan village.

By April 1805 the expedition, having already collected a large number of scientific specimens, Native American objects, mineral samples, animal skins, and live animals, including a prairie dog, decided to send about a dozen men back downriver so that the initial discoveries could be presented to

Native American hunting party. The Corps of Discovery encountered many different Native American tribes, from whom were collected all manner of artefacts. (Library of Congress Prints and Photographs Division)

the president. The remaining 33 members of the expedition, with two boats and six dugout canoes, prepared to proceed west, aware that 2,000 miles (3,219km) still lay between them and the Pacific. By the end of the month they were deep into present-day Montana, where, as Lewis noted in his diary, they encountered "herds of Buffaloe, Elk, deer, Antelopes feeding in one common and boundless pasture." The party carefully mapped its route, sometimes encountering hostile grizzly bears – another species not known in the east. Lewis observed in his journal that "the Indians give a very formidable account of the strength and ferocity of this animal, which they never dare to attack but in parties of six, eight or ten persons; and are even then frequently defeated with the loss of one or more of their party."

On June 2, the expedition encountered a fork in the river, causing speculation as to the true course of the Missouri. Eleven days later Lewis, having proceeded ahead in

search of an answer, discovered the Great Falls, thus confirming his theory as to the river's true origins. When he later encountered four more waterfalls just upriver, the expedition was forced to make an arduous overland diversion of nearly 20 miles (32km) to circumvent them, the men hauling their canoes and supplies in the summer heat.

By mid-August the expedition was in Shoshone territory, near the border of what is now Montana and Idaho, where Lewis hoped to find the Northwest Passage, the existence of which generations of previous explorers believed could shorten the journey to the Pacific. But there was no great body of water: only more mountains. From the Shoshone Lewis and Clark acquired horses for the journey over the mountains, and by the end of the month the expedition, now mounted, proceeded on its journey across the Continental Divide. By mid-September, the expedition, suffering from near-starvation and plunging temperatures,

had reached the heavily wooded Bitterroot Mountains, which took an agonizing 11 days to cross. Emerging near what is now Weippe, Idaho, the expedition encountered friendly Native Americans known as the Nez Percé, who showed the explorers how to hollow out trees with fire to make canoes.

With these the expedition proceeded rapidly down the Clearwater and Snake Rivers, reaching the salmon-choked Columbia. When, on October 18, Clark excitedly made out Mount Hood, a landmark sited by the British in 1792, he was aware that the Pacific was close. Plunging into the forests of the Pacific Northwest, the expedition, after a journey of over 4,000 miles (6,437km), was at last within reach of the ocean, though foul weather held up their

Native Americans hunting buffalo. In his journal, Lewis made numerous references to massive herds of these magnificent beasts, whose meat the members of the expedition would eagerly devour as an alternative to fish. (Library of Congress Prints and Photographs Division)

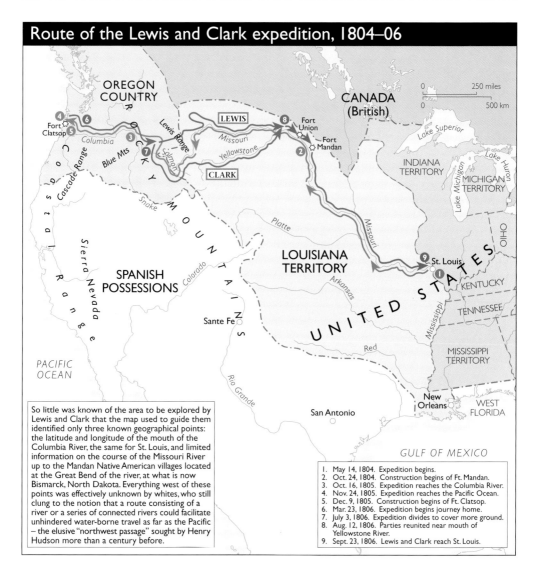

Route of the Lewis and Clark expedition, 1804–06

So little was known of the area to be explored by Lewis and Clark that the map used to guide them identified only three known geographical points: the latitude and longitude of the mouth of the Columbia River, the same for St. Louis, and limited information on the course of the Missouri River up to the Mandan Native American villages located at the Great Bend of the river, at what is now Bismarck, North Dakota. Everything west of these points was effectively unknown by whites, who still clung to the notion that a route consisting of a river or a series of connected rivers could facilitate unhindered water-borne travel as far as the Pacific – the elusive "northwest passage" sought by Henry Hudson more than a century before.

1. May 14, 1804. Expedition begins.
2. Oct. 24, 1804. Construction begins of Ft. Mandan.
3. Oct. 16, 1805. Expedition reaches the Columbia River.
4. Nov. 24, 1805. Expedition reaches the Pacific Ocean.
5. Dec. 9, 1805. Construction begins of Ft. Clatsop.
6. Mar. 23, 1806. Expedition begins journey home.
7. July 3, 1806. Expedition divides to cover more ground.
8. Aug. 12, 1806. Parties reunited near mouth of Yellowstone River.
9. Sept. 23, 1806. Lewis and Clark reach St. Louis.

progress for almost three weeks. The Pacific proved less calm than was expected, as Lewis explained in his journal: "Since we arrived in Sight of the Great Western Ocian, I cant Say Pasific as Since I have seen it, it has been the reverse [sic]." The expedition established winter quarters called Fort Clatsop, near what is now Astoria, Oregon, and settled down until spring.

After a cold and rainy winter, the expedition proceeded on the long journey home, which began on March 23, 1806. Waiting for the snow to melt, the men crossed the Bitterroots before the expedition divided on July 3 in order to cover more

ground. As Clark moved down the Yellowstone River, Lewis proceeded along the Marias River. Clark reached the Yellowstone in late July and re-entered the Great Plains in present-day Montana. Lewis, meanwhile, encountered a group of Blackfeet, two of whom he shot and killed as they attempted to steal his party's horses and guns. He then proceeded toward the rendezvous with Clark, and by August 12 the expedition was at last reunited.

Finally, on September 23, 1806, the Corps of Discovery – long since given up for dead – reached St. Louis, two and a half years after having set off. Lewis and Clark then made

Pioneers moving west. Although this phenomenon took time to gather pace, the westward trek of thousands of American settlers was a direct result of the Corps of Discovery's trailblazing expedition at the turn of the 19th century.
(Library of Congress Prints and Photographs Division)

their way to Washington, hailed as heroes as they went, their achievement celebrated across the country. Enthusiastically received by the president, Congress, and the capital's residents, these most accomplished explorers in American history were handsomely rewarded with land, money, and appointments, Lewis being made governor of the Louisiana Territory, and Clark appointed Indian agent for the West. In the course of the journey, the expedition had suffered only one casualty, and returned with descriptions of over 100 animals and nearly 200 plants hitherto unknown Having mapped a course to the Pacific, Lewis and Clark had paved the way for the settlement of America's vast new hinterland.

John Foss: white slave in Algiers

On October 25, 1793, the *Polly*, hailing from Baltimore and two days' sail from Cadiz, in southern Spain, sighted an unidentified vessel. Captain Samuel Bayley and the eight members of his crew believed the ship to be a British privateer, and as the United States and Britain were then at peace, all seemed well. When the mysterious ship approached the *Polly* the British flag was seen flying aloft, and when she came alongside a lone man on deck wearing Western dress hailed the American brig. But all was not well; as Foss recalled in his book, once the unnamed vessel lay by the stern of the *Polly*, the unsuspecting Americans:

… saw a great number of men rise up with their heads above the gunnel, drest [sic] in the Turkish habit … They immediately hoisted out a large launch, and about one hundred of the Pirates jumped on board, all armed, some with Scimitres [sic] and Pistols, others with pikes, spears, lances, knives, &c … As soon as they came on board our vessel, they made signs for us all to go forward, assuring us in several languages, that if we did not obey their command, they would immediately massacre us all.

The Americans were immediately stripped of most of their clothes and taken aboard the Algerine vessel, where they were thrown into the hold, there to encounter "vermin, such as lice, bugs, and fleas … in such quantity that it seemed as if we were entirely covered with those unwelcome guests." They were unable to sleep, for "our minds were filled with horror, and dreadful apprehensions of the fate we might experience, and expecting additional severity on our arrival at Algiers."

Sailing through the Strait of Gibraltar, Foss and his compatriots reached Algiers where they landed:

… amidst the shouts and huzzas of thousands of malicious barbarians. We were conducted to the Dey's palace by a guard, and as we passed through the streets, our ears were stunned with the shouts, clapping of hands, and other acclamations of joy from the inhabitants, thanking God for their great success, and victories over so many Christian dogs, and unbelievers, which is the appellation they generally give to all Christians.

The dey announced to his captives the impossibility of peace with the United States, adding ominously: "Now I have got you, Christian dogs, you shall eat stones."

Foss and the others were conducted to a *bagnio*, or prison, where they discovered 600 other captives, "all appearing to be in a more miserable condition than ourselves, with wretched habits, dejected countenances, and chains on their legs, every part of them bespeaking unutterable distress." Their names recorded in a book as a guard stood by, stick in hand, each prisoner then received a small bundle containing a blanket, jacket, waistcoat, collarless shirt, a pair of trousers, and a pair of slippers. This constituted a prisoner's yearly supply of clothing. The meal Foss received, together with his compatriots, consisted of a small loaf of sour black bread, weighing about 3½oz (100g). He slept on a stone floor without bedding of any kind. At 3.00am he and the other men were roused from sleep and a length of chain weighing between 25 and 40lb (11 and 18kg) was placed around each man's leg. Then Foss and some of the other prisoners were taken to the marina, where he:

experienced the hardest day's work I ever underwent before. The dreadful clanking of chains was the most terrible noise I ever heard.

placed them on sleds and hauled them the 2 miles (3.2km) to the quay. The guards made no allowance for the physical exhaustion of the miserable laborers, as Foss relates:

They [the slaves] must haul as many [sleds] in a day as the task-masters think proper, and are treated with additional rigor and severity on this day. For the drivers being anxious to have as many hauled as possible … they are continually beating the slaves with their sticks, and goading them with its end, in which is a small spear, not unlike an ox goad, among our farmers. If anyone chance[s] to faint, and fall[s] down with fatigue, they generally beat them until they are able to rise again.

Once the rocks were dragged to the harbor, they were loaded onto large flat-bottomed boats, floated to the back of the mole, and dumped overboard to form a breakwater. The great irony of this whole ghastly exercise was that this exceedingly laborious task had no end, for gales and wind continually washed the rocks forming the breakwater into deeper water, requiring the mole to be repaired and enlarged on a regular basis.

Still other slaves assigned to work in the harbor cleaned the corsairs and merchant vessels, prepared them for sea, and unloaded their cargoes on their return. A contingent of slaves conveyed into the city the goods brought in by ship and, conversely, carried supplies and goods from the city to be loaded on to ships in the harbor, a task performed by the men with the aid of poles resting on their shoulders. Many streets were so narrow as to be impassable not merely to wheeled vehicles, but to two people walking abreast. Slaves carried such items as hogsheads of sugar, jugs of liquid, and casks of nails, and were searched before they returned to the prison to ensure that nothing had been stolen.

Slaves too sick to work were sent to a hospital established by the Spanish centuries before, but patients were immediately expelled and returned to work when a "task-master" dictated it, without consultation with the doctors. Such prisoners

A slave's head set alight, either as a punishment or for the simple amusement of onlookers. This and other late 17th-century engravings caused revulsion and outcry throughout Europe, where, on the other hand, torture was still widely practiced and only recently abolished in England under Cromwell. (James Ford Bell Library, University of Minnesota)

And never during my whole captivity did I feel such horrors of mind, as on this dreadful [first] morning.

Foss, like so many other slaves, was regularly sent to the port to build and repair breakwaters and fortifications. Many slaves struggled to break up rocks in the mountains that loomed up behind Algiers, drilling holes, digging out the earth from between the rocks, and carrying away the soil to the harbor to be used as landfill. Massive boulders weighing as much as 40 tons (36 tonnes), were hewn from the mountainside, then rolled down the mountain to the bottom, where other slaves often collapsed from exhaustion within a few hours, sometimes to die shortly thereafter. Foss recalled how one such man "did the best he could for about half an hour, and then fell down insensible. Upon this he was again sent to the hospital, expired at two o'clock in the afternoon, & was in his grave before sunset."

At night Foss and the other slaves assembled for roll call. They were then conducted back to the gates of the city, where they were required to find their own way back to the prison. A slave who failed to reach his quarters by the appointed time, or who neglected to answer to his name when roll was repeated inside, was chained to a pillar by his hands and feet. In the morning his irons were removed and he received an additional punishment, usually between 100 and 200 bastinadoes. Foss described the procedure thus:

... the person is laid upon his face, with his hands in irons behind him and his legs lashed together with a rope. One task-master holds down his head and another his legs, while two others inflict the punishment upon his breech, with sticks, some what larger than an ox goad. After he has received one half in this manner, they lash his ancles [sic] to a pole, and two Turks lift the pole up, and hold it in such a manner, as brings the soles of his feet upward, and the remainder of his punishment he receives upon the soles of his feet. Then he is released from his bands, and obliged to go directly to work among the rest of his fellow slaves.

Punishments for slaves varied according to the nature of their infraction. For theft they could be burned at the stake or impaled. "This is done," Foss wrote, "by placing the criminal upon a sharp iron stake, and thrusting it up his posteriors, by his back bone 'till it appears at the back of his neck." For the murder of another slave, the man was immediately beheaded. If he murdered a Muslim, however:

he is cast off from the walls of the city, upon iron hooks, which are fastened into the wall

about half way down. These catch by any part of the body that strikes them, and some times they hang in this manner in the most exquisite agonies for several days before they expire. But should the part that catches not be strong enough to hold them (for sometimes the flesh will tear out), they fall to the bottom of the wall and are dashed in pieces.

An equally dreadful fate awaited a prisoner if he attempted to escape. In that case, Foss recorded – though never having witnessed it himself – the offender is "nailed to the gallows, by one hand and opposite foot, and in this manner they expire, in the most indescribable torture. But this is not always practiced for desertion, for sometimes they are only bastinadoed, at other times they are beheaded."

Foss' captivity slowly turned from months to years, with little variation in his daily routine. At 8.00am he was given breakfast, consisting of nothing more than a small loaf of bread, a bowl of vinegar, and a cup of water, which he was expected to eat, whilst sitting on the ground, in ten minutes. The same ration was repeated at about noon, and again at night. In all, the daily allowance of bread weighed under a pound, and was "so sour," Foss recalled, "that a person must be almost starving before he can eat it."

At night Foss and the other slaves slept in dreadful quarters, the prison consisting of several galleries built one above the other, each gallery divided into several small rooms. The prison also housed "a great number of animals of prey ... confined with chains in different apartments from where the slaves sleep." Some prisoners were assigned to feed these beasts – presumably lions and wolves – with cow and sheep heads. Under such conditions, Foss was fortunate to avoid contracting smallpox and the plague, though he and other eyewitnesses recorded numerous instances of such diseases amongst fellow captives, some of whom died from infection.

Any prospect of relief from his sufferings did not come for Foss until two and a half years into his captivity when, in March

Hot wax being applied to the soles of a slave's feet. The treatment of a prisoner varied according to the whim of his master. Cervantes, who witnessed various cruelties being inflicted by slave owners, claimed of one: "Every day he hanged a slave, and cut the ears off another. He did it merely for the sake of doing it." (James Ford Bell Library, University of Minnesota)

Execution of slaves by crucifixion, burning at the stake, and suspension on hooks from the city walls. (James Ford Bell Library, University of Minnesota)

1796, a brig flying the Stars and Stripes and bearing the new US consul-general, Joel Barlow, appeared in the harbor of Algiers. Seeking to secure the release of the American prisoners, Barlow sent a letter to the captives, assuring them that:

… you are neither forgotten [n]or neglected by your country … Impossibilities cannot be effected: But whatever is in its nature practicable will be done in your behalf. Let me therefore, my dear Countrymen … exhort you to be of good courage, to exert all your fortitude, to have a little more patience, to hope always for the best, and to be persuaded that every thing is doing and shall be done, which the nature of circumstances will admit, for your relief.

For the prisoners, the period of ensuing negotiations moved painfully slowly. At last, on July 11, after their ransom had been paid, Foss and the other Americans in Algerine hands were duly released, though only three other men from the *Polly* had survived the ordeal, and, by a cruel irony, Captain Bayley would die of the plague a few days after being freed. After encountering various dangers in a long, circuitous, and eventful journey home, Foss finally reached his hometown of Newburyport, Massachusetts, on August 23, 1797. He was one of the lucky ones, for he estimated that 1,200 slaves of various nationalities still remained in Algiers.

The Algerine Wars (1815–16) and the French expedition to North Africa (1830)

The US Navy returns to the Mediterranean

After 1805 a period of relative inactivity, so far as piracy was concerned, followed in the Mediterranean. The conflict then raging in Europe drastically reduced commercial traffic, and Nelson's victory at Trafalgar on October 21 confirmed Britain's naval dominance in that sea, thus enabling the Royal Navy to restrict or interdict neutral or hostile trade destined for a continent largely under French control. As the Barbary States knew better than to prey on British merchant vessels and those of Britain's allies, relations remained on an amicable footing. Still, American ships continued to be harassed and occasionally seized, not least after the United States became preoccupied with its war with Britain, which began in June 1812. From that point, America was in no position to defend its citizens thousands of miles from home; specifically, the very limited resources of the Navy were required in the Atlantic.

During the war, the US Navy – in sharp contrast to the appalling record of the Army – acquitted itself exceedingly well. Without ships of the line, America could not shake off the blockade of its eastern seaboard. Yet in numerous frigate actions both at sea and on the Great Lakes, the Navy consistently bested its British opponents in a virtually unbroken catalog of victories, many achieved by veterans of the Tripolitan War. Thus, when the war against Britain ended with the Treaty of Ghent on December 24, 1814, both President Madison and Congress felt confident that the United States possessed the means to face the Barbary States, reassert

the nation's right to free trade, and put a final end to their depredations and insults to the American flag. The Navy could no longer call on the services of Preble, who had died of tuberculosis in 1807, but many of his subordinates from the heady days of 1804, now experienced captains, were once again available for service in the Mediterranean. Thus, on February 23, 1815, with the Anglo-American treaty ratified and the Navy's exploits fresh in his mind, Madison sent a message to Congress requesting a declaration of war on Algiers. Congress obliged on March 2.

The Navy duly dispatched two squadrons, each led by a veteran of the war against Tripoli: one from Boston under Bainbridge, and the other from New York under Decatur. Decatur departed on May 20 aboard his flagship, *Guerrière* (44 guns), with two other frigates, *Macedonian* (38) and *Constellation* (36); the sloops *Epervier* (18) and *Ontario* (16); the brigs *Firefly*, *Spark*, and *Flambeau*, each of 14 guns; and the schooners *Torch* and *Spitfire*, mounting 12 guns each. With this respectable force went the new consul-general to the Barbary States, William Shaler, who was to reside in Algiers.

Decatur arrived at Gibraltar on June 15; two days later, on the morning of the 17th, the *Constellation* sighted a large Algerine frigate. Decatur immediately pursued, bringing the *Guerrière* so close to the 46-gun *Mashouda* that the Algerines issued musketry from her tops, wounding several Americans. Maneuvering alongside the *Mashouda*, Decatur fired a broadside, causing considerable damage. The Algerine captain, Reis Hammida, was already wounded from a shot fired from the *Constellation* and was sitting on his quarterdeck directing operations. He was not to do so for long: a 42lb (19kg) shot fired from one of the *Guerrière*'s carronades soon cut him in two. The thunderous crash of a second broadside then drove the Algerines below, apart from a determined few standing on the top deck and perched in the rigging who continued to issue musket fire. Now the *Epervier* came up on the enemy's starboard quarter, firing broadside after broadside, eventually forcing the battered Algerine ship to bring her head to the wind and surrender. Decatur took 406 prisoners, many of them wounded, and sent the prize, escorted by the *Macedonian*, to Cartagena. The *Guerrière* lost one seaman killed and three wounded as a result of enemy fire, and three killed and seven wounded from a bursting gun. The commodore followed up his success on June 19, when off Cape Palos his squadron chased the 22-gun brig *Estedio*, forcing her aground. Some of the crew escaped to the shore in boats, one of which was sunk, but of the remaining Algerines about 80 surrendered.

As the squadron approached Algiers, Decatur held a council of his captains, to whom he expressed the hope that the dey would submit to terms and avoid further bloodshed. If, however, the American ultimatum was refused, the squadron would attack the batteries and shipping in the harbor. The squadron arrived off the city on June 28. The following morning Decatur, by way of indicating his wish to negotiate through the Swedish consul, Norderling, hoisted a white flag atop the foremast of his flagship and Swedish colors at the main. A letter from the president, dated April 12, was sent ashore, stating that the United States had declared war on Algiers and expressing the hope that the dey, Omar Pasha, would agree to American peace terms or suffer the consequences. If the dey chose peace, ran the letter, it could only be durable if "founded on stipulations equally beneficial to both parties, the one claiming nothing which it is not willing to grant to the other; and on this basis alone will its attainment or preservation by this government be

desirable." Accompanying this was a second, equally firm letter, signed by Decatur and Shaler, and dated June 29, which warned that "they are instructed to treat upon no other principle than that of perfect equality on the terms of the most favored nations. No stipulation for paying any tribute to Algiers under any form whatever will be agreed to."

Decatur, determined to show a strong hand from the outset, refused to go ashore to negotiate, instead insisting that all talks be conducted aboard the *Guerrière*, and warning that any Algerine vessels that attempted to enter or leave the harbor before the conclusion of peace would be seized or sunk. Talks began on the 30th, the Americans presenting a draft treaty to the Swedish consul and the dey's representative. The terms were blunt: tribute was to cease entirely; American captives in Algiers were immediately to be released; Decatur would in turn release his recently captured prisoners; the dey would pay $10,000 in compensation for the ship *Edwin* and other American property recently seized by the Algerines; finally, the dey was to promise that in any future conflict with the United States all captives were to be treated humanely, and not forced to work as slaves.

The Algerines requested a truce until peace could be formally concluded; this the Americans categorically rejected. Nor would Decatur wait the three hours requested by the dey's commissioner to consider the terms, with or without a ceasefire. "Not a minute," the commodore replied, repeating his threat to fire upon and capture any Algerine vessel that attempted to enter or leave the harbor.

With these uncompromising words, the dey's commissioner went ashore, returning three hours later in a boat flying a white flag, bearing a signed copy of the treaty, and all ten of the dey's American prisoners. Reporting to the secretary of the navy on July 5, Decatur wrote that peace:

... has been dictated at the mouths of our cannon, has been conceded [owing] to the losses which Algiers has sustained [the Mashouda *and*

USS *Constitution* exchanges broadsides with HMS *Guerrière*, August 19, 1812. Captain Isaac Hull thoroughly drubbed his British opponent off the coast of Nova Scotia in one of a long series of brilliant American frigate actions fought during the War of 1812. The captured *Guerrière* served as Decatur's flagship in 1815. (Public Domain)

Estedio*], and to the dread of still greater evils apprehended. And I beg leave to express to you my opinion that the presence of a respectable naval force in this sea will be the only certain guarantee for its observance.*

Later the same day, Shaler went ashore and returned to the *Guerrière* bearing the $10,000 stipulated in the treaty, as well as property belonging to the liberated slaves. The dey's minister, distraught at the speed of events, complained bitterly to the British consul: "You told us that the Americans would be swept from the seas in six months by your navy, and now they make war upon us with some of your own vessels which they have taken [i.e. the *Guerrière*, captured from the British in 1812]."

The treaty, achieved in less than six weeks after Decatur's departure from New York, represented a remarkable diplomatic success for the United States. It was clearly the most favorable treaty ever concluded by a Western nation with Algiers, and marked the beginning of the end of both piracy and white slavery in North Africa. The *Epervier*, dispatched to carry the treaty to the United

States, passed Gibraltar on July 12, but was lost somewhere in the Atlantic, speculation being that she sank in a gale known to have occurred off the American coast around the time the sloop was expected to reach port.

Meanwhile, Decatur departed from Algiers on July 8, taking on fresh water and provisions at Sardinia, before proceeding to Tunis, where he dropped anchor on the 26th. After consultation with the American consul there, Decatur demanded an immediate payment of $46,000 in compensation for two British vessels – originally taken as prizes by an American privateer during the recent conflict – seized in port by the bey. Mahmud, the bey of Tunis, yielded to American demands and, after a brief show of complaint, surrendered the money to the American consul.

Decatur thereupon left Tunis for Tripoli, where he arrived three days later. With his ships cleared for action, as at Tunis he demanded $30,000 in compensation for British ships taken as prizes into Tripoli by American privateers, but subsequently confiscated by government officials. The pasha was also informed of the terms recently imposed on Tunis and Algiers. The Tripolitans eventually settled on $25,000, which the American consul suggested was the more accurate value of the two vessels concerned, but Decatur only agreed to this reduced figure

on condition that the pasha release ten of his European captives. Eight Sicilians – a husband, wife, and six children – plus two Danes, were taken aboard the American squadron, together with the agreed payment in gold.

On August 9, having successfully completed his mission, Decatur left Tripoli, and after touching at several Neapolitan and Spanish ports and finally Gibraltar, he arrived on November 12 at New York, where he was rapturously received by the public. In Washington, the Madison administration offered its grateful thanks, while Congress went even further, appropriating $100,000 to be divided between Decatur, his officers, and men for the two seized Algerine ships, notwithstanding the fact that those vessels had been restored to the dey in accordance with the terms of the recently concluded treaty.

Bainbridge, commanding the second squadron destined for the Mediterranean, had left Boston on July 3 with part of his force, the remainder joining him later, including the first American ship of the line in the Mediterranean, the 74-gun *Independence*. Bainbridge called first at Algiers, then Tripoli, and finally Tunis, to show the flag and to reaffirm America's resolve no longer to tolerate the harassment of its nationals, its refusal henceforth to revert to its tributary status, and its condemnation of the practice of white

Decatur's squadron off Algiers, June 1815. Hereafter, the United States saw fit to leave a squadron on permanent station in the Mediterranean to protect American interests. For the next 15 years presidential messages almost invariably made reference to the wisdom of continuing this policy. (Mariners' Museum, Newport News, Virginia)

slavery. The appearance of a second powerful squadron in the immediate wake of the first succeeded in its purpose to the extent that thereafter Barbary corsairs ceased to prey on American ships, insurance coming in the form of a small US squadron left permanently on station in the Mediterranean to protect American commerce and to enforce the terms to which the Barbary States had agreed.

Satisfactory though this state of affairs may have appeared to the United States, it offered no consolation to the thousands of European slaves who still languished in prisons and galleys across North Africa. Only one European state possessed the means to liberate them: Britain.

The Royal Navy follows suit

On January 22, 1816, the USS *Java* left Newport, Rhode Island, carrying the ratified treaty with Algiers. As the frigate approached that city, with its citadel and minarets towering above all else, the crew sighted a sizeable British squadron lying at anchor. Encouraged by Decatur's success, the British had come to negotiate their own terms on behalf of various European powers whose nationals remained in captivity. But the dey, stung by his recent agreement with the Americans, was in no mood to receive the British with open arms, as the captain of the *Java* explained in a letter home: "The Algerines are extremely restive under the treaty made with Decatur, considering it disgraceful to the Faithful to humble themselves before Christian dogs." Leading the British expedition was Sir Edward Pellew, Lord Exmouth, who had been commander-in-chief of the Mediterranean Fleet in the final years of the Napoleonic Wars, which had only concluded six months previously, the battle of Waterloo having been fought the day after Decatur had captured the *Mashouda*.

Several factors contributed to Britain's interest in suppressing Barbary piracy. First,

Decatur and the dey of Algiers on the deck of the USS *Guerrière*. The American commodore arrived on the Barbary coast in no mood to compromise, and the symbolism behind his command of a former British warship cannot have been lost on his host. (New York Public Library Picture Collection)

the end of hostilities with France no longer necessitated a substantial Royal Navy presence in the Mediterranean, which meant that the demand for victuals, water and supplies from North Africa fell accordingly, so ending the necessity for Britain to remain on good terms with the Barbary States. Second, the Barbary States ceased to be useful both in commercial terms and as irritants to Britain's wartime adversaries. Third, the end of the war in Europe opened the Mediterranean once again to a large volume of merchant traffic which, if left unescorted, stood vulnerable to piracy. Fourth, the subject of slavery and the slave trade had arisen at the Congress of Vienna, which had convened in the autumn of 1814 to settle the political affairs of Europe. Specifically, Lord Castlereagh, the British foreign secretary, had tabled – amongst many other more pressing issues – the question of the abolition of black slavery, condemning it on moral grounds. Britain had herself abolished the *trade* in slaves within the Empire in 1807, though the *practice* of slavery continued in the West Indies. This meant that slave-owners were free to continue to exploit slave labor on their plantations in Jamaica and elsewhere, but they could not import new slaves from Africa. Discussion of black slavery in the Americas naturally renewed interest in the question of the eradication of white slavery in North Africa, a problem that, owing to Europe's preoccupation with war until the fall of Napoleon, had remained unresolved.

With this question in mind, the British government, led by Lord Liverpool, dispatched Exmouth to the Mediterranean, there to call at the various Barbary States. Acting as an intermediary on behalf of various minor European powers that had solicited Britain's aid, Exmouth was instructed to secure the release of the unknown number of European slaves still in captivity. Most of these were believed to come from Spain, Corsica, the various Italian states, and the Ionian Islands, protection over the last of which the Congress of Vienna had granted to Britain. Exmouth was cautioned against using force, at least not initially, for fear the slaves could be massacred in retaliation. Instead, the admiral was to offer ransom in return for the prisoners' freedom. Appreciating that the Barbary States might reject his proposals, Exmouth sent Captains Warde and Pechell to reconnoiter Algiers and Tunis, respectively, and submit a detailed report on the state of their defenses. If circumstances warranted, the British squadron would resort to bombardment, with Algiers, the most aggressive state, the likeliest target.

Exmouth arrived off Algiers on March 24, 1816, with five ships of the line and seven frigates and sloops. The dey appeared amenable to negotiation, and accepted 1,000 Spanish dollars a head for his Sicilian and Neapolitan prisoners, with the Genoese and Sardinians released at half this rate. The dey also agreed to peace with the various European states with which he was at war, though, significantly, no discussion took place as to the question of piracy in general.

Exmouth next sailed to Tunis, where he arrived on April 12, and proceeded to demonstrate great firmness backed by the menace of his warships, not least because a Tunisian corsair had recently raided an island off Sardinia, producing widespread indignation across Europe. Exmouth found the bey reluctant to accede to his terms. British merchants hurried to take refuge aboard the warships, which lay offshore preparing for a fight, while the bey, Mahmud, for his part ordered the assembly of reinforcements for the defense of the city, whose inhabitants daily grew more excited by the prospect of a confrontation. Exmouth's difficulties were increased by the chance presence in Tunis of the Prince Regent's estranged wife, Caroline, Princess of Wales – a guest, no less, residing in the bey's palace. Caroline feared she would be taken hostage, in spite of assurances from the bey that she would come to no harm under the protection of his hospitality. Meanwhile, at the British consulate, the flag was lowered to half mast to indicate a resolution to fight should the talks fail.

Bloodshed was indeed averted; on the 16th, Exmouth, together with the Consul-General Oglander and his staff, went to the Bardo Palace and opened negotiations. The following day the two sides concluded a treaty: the bey released 524 slaves in exchange for payment, while 257 others were freed at no cost. He also agreed that any future captives would be treated as prisoners of war and not forced to work as slaves.

Satisfied with his work at Tunis, Exmouth next proceeded to Tripoli, where he not only secured the release of 468 slaves in exchange for 50,000 Spanish dollars, but received a promise from Yusuf Karamanli (still pasha a decade after the Tripolitan War) that he would abolish slavery altogether.

This further success convinced Exmouth to return to Algiers to seek the same promise from the government there. Despite lengthy discussions in May, Exmouth failed to extract the desired promise, the dey offering only great defiance. As tension mounted in the palace, ill-feeling grew manifest in the streets of the city, where two of Exmouth's officers were unhorsed by a mob and marched through the city with their hands tied behind their backs. Algerine officials placed the British consul, McDonnell, under house arrest, while his wife and family were ejected from their country residence and forced back to the capital. On top of these insults, the dey insisted that he required authority from Constantinople to conclude a new treaty; six months were therefore required for an answer from the sultan.

Exmouth possessed no instructions from the Admiralty with which to cope with these contingencies. Thus frustrated, the admiral left Algiers and reached Spithead on June 24, having achieved nothing more than persuading the Algerines to dispatch an envoy to London. In the meantime, the dey assumed that war had broken out with Britain and prepared his defenses accordingly.

Hardly was Exmouth back in London to submit a report on his mission to his superiors than news arrived of the massacre – reputedly on the dey's orders – of 200 Italian

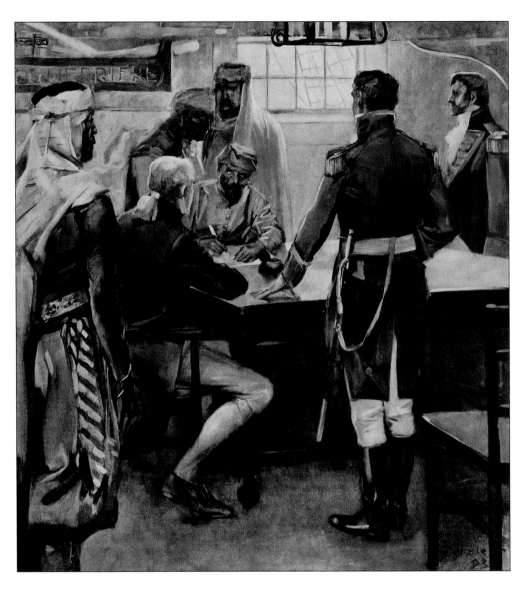

The fruits of gunboat diplomacy. A Barbary official signs a treaty of peace with the United States in the captain's cabin of the *Guerrière*. When, barely a century later, Theodore Roosevelt used the fleet for similar purposes, he was merely continuing a tradition begun by his presidential predecessor, James Madison, in 1815. (New York Public Library Picture Collection)

fishermen in the Algerine coastal towns of Bona and Oran. Public outrage in Britain, compounded by widespread criticism of what many regarded as the government's lenient treatment of the Barbary States, effectively obliged Lord Liverpool to send a new, more powerful, squadron to the

Mediterranean. Sailing from Portsmouth on July 24, Exmouth bore orders to seek redress from Algiers, by force if necessary.

Nothing in the composition of the squadron suggested conciliatory intentions. It consisted of the three-deckers *Queen Charlotte* (100 guns), which was Exmouth's flagship, and the *Impregnable* (98), under Rear-Admiral David Milne. With these were three 74s: the *Superb*, *Minden*, and *Albion*, and two frigates of 40 guns each, the *Severn* and *Glasgow*, plus two 36-gun frigates, the *Granicus* and *Hebrus*, five sloops, and four bomb-vessels. Exmouth left port with part of this force and joined the remainder at Plymouth. He was to have been joined at Gibraltar by Admiral Penrose, but unaccountably that officer never received instructions to this effect. Nevertheless, when he reached the Rock, Exmouth found a Dutch squadron of five frigates, mostly of 36 guns each, and a corvette, under Admiral Theodore Van de Capellan, who gratuitously offered his assistance.

Exmouth gratefully accepted this unexpected reinforcement, at the same time augmenting his own force by requisitioning extra supplies of powder, fitting special sights to the guns, and ordering extra gunnery practice for the crews. Launches were armed with carronades (very large-caliber ordnance used at close-range), flat-bottomed boats were fitted out to launch Congreve rockets, and a sloop was converted into an explosion vessel with 143 barrels of gunpowder on board. On weighing anchor, this enlarged squadron had now effectively become a fleet, with a combined strength of 35 vessels.

Fortunately for Exmouth, he was well-acquainted with the defenses of Algiers. Apart from having himself twice visited the city, he possessed intelligence from Warde, including soundings taken in the harbor and an estimate of the number of guns mounted in the forts. Despite these advantages, there was no possibility of a surprise attack; the dey's corsairs gave him advance warning of his enemy's approach.

The task before Exmouth was a formidable one: to destroy the batteries in the harbor and force the dey to accept British terms. When on August 27 the fleet arrived in the roads of Algiers, Exmouth sent in the *Prometheus* to convey an ultimatum and to carry back, by stealth, the British consul, McDonnell, and his family. McDonnell's wife and daughter arrived safely in one boat, but a second was intercepted by the Algerines when the family's baby cried out. McDonnell, his infant, and the boat crew were brought before the dey, who had the baby sent to its mother, but detained the rest of the group.

When no reply was forthcoming to Exmouth's ultimatum, the admiral hoisted the signal for battle, and action began at

Sir Edward Pellew, 1st Viscount Exmouth. His service in the Royal Navy stretched back to the American Revolutionary War, though he did not hold senior command until the French Revolutionary and Napoleonic Wars, at the end of which he served as commander-in-chief of the Mediterranean Fleet (1811–14). (Philip Haythornthwaite)

2.00pm. Leading the column was the admiral in the *Queen Charlotte*, which penetrated so far into the harbor that when she came to anchor only 80 yards (73m) from the shore, only 2ft (0.6m) of water remained under her keel. Were she to become grounded, *the Queen Charlotte* would, like the *Philadelphia* in 1804, stand little chance of saving herself. As per instructions, the *Leander* proceeded past the flagship, and at just before 3.00pm the fish-market battery began to fire, the British replying with simultaneous broadsides from the *Queen Charlotte* and *Leander*. Characterizing the fight in moralistic terms, Exmouth wrote in his dispatch following the action:

Then commenced a fire as animated and well-supported as I believe was ever witnessed … The ships immediately following me were admirably and coolly taking up their

stations, with a precision even beyond my most sanguine hope; and never did the British flag receive, on any occasion, more zealous and honourable support.

The battle was fairly at issue between a handful of Britons, in the noble cause of Christianity, and a horde of fanatics, assembled round their city, and enclosed within its fortifications, to obey the dictates of their Despot.

The exchange of fire, which was to rage without interruption for the next six hours, created so much noise as to be heard over 50 miles (80km) away. The *Severn* and *Glasgow* assumed their intended positions, as did the Dutch frigates, but the *Superb* anchored 200 yards (183m) away from her appointed place, leaving twice the distance between herself and the batteries she was meant to engage. Milne's massive three-decker, the *Impregnable*, was far too slow and finally anchored 400 yards (366m) out of position and within easy reach of the lighthouse battery, so deviating from Exmouth's plan. The *Minden* anchored astern of the *Superb*. The *Albion* first dropped anchor ahead of the *Impregnable* before proceeding slightly astern of the *Minden*. The unintended gap astern of the *Queen Charlotte* was taken up by the frigate *Granicus* and the sloop *Heron* – brave acts for such vessels since, being smaller and more vulnerable than their mightier consorts, they were not meant to occupy a place in the line of battle.

The *Queen Charlotte*, being the most heavily armed vessel, made easy work of the batteries near her, silencing their guns in less than half an hour. The *Impregnable*, with fewer guns and of smaller caliber, fought for hours with considerably less effect. At 4.00pm, the British burned the enemy vessel moored across the mouth of the harbor and half an hour later the squadron took up positions in order to bombard the harbor and town. At approximately 8.00pm, Exmouth directed the explosion vessel to be deployed against the lighthouse battery so as to divert the enemy's attention from the beleaguered *Impregnable*. At 9.10pm the explosion vessel blew up – near the wrong

battery – and with disappointing results. Still, by this point the Algerine fleet, such as it was, had been annihilated, and as the firing faded away in the darkness Exmouth issued the signal for the squadron to break off the action and withdraw. Firing ceased altogether when the *Minden*, covering the withdrawal, expended the last of her ammunition around 11.30pm. Behind her many of the enemy's guns lay dismounted from their carriages, surrounded by shattered masonry and the bodies of the gunners which had faithfully manned them.

The *Queen Charlotte* finally dropped anchor at 1.30am, her crew – as with those aboard all the other ships in the fleet – utterly exhausted after the day's heavy work at the guns. "The cause of God and humanity prevailed," Exmouth proudly declared in his report to the Admiralty, "and so devoted was every creature in the fleet, that even British women served at the same guns with their husbands, and, during a contest of many hours, never shrank from danger, but animated all around them." Every enemy ship in port was on fire, which "… extended rapidly over the whole arsenal, storehouses, and gun-boats, exhibiting a spectacle of awful grandeur and interest no pen can describe." The presence of heavy thunder, lightning, and rain rendered the scene all the more dramatic. Upon waking the following morning and surveying the devastation, Shaler observed: "Lord Exmouth holds the fate of Algiers in his hands."

And so he did. At noon that day a messenger bearing a flag of truce went ashore and conveyed a letter addressed by the admiral to the dey, repeating the terms originally offered. Should the dey fail to comply, Exmouth's note ran, "I shall renew my operations at my own convenience." Three Algerine guns boomed out as a signal for acceptance, and when the negotiations came to an end the dey not only released 1,642 slaves – the majority of these were Italians, although there were also 18 British subjects – but repaid the money previously given to him to free the prisoners, publicly apologized to McDonnell (who had been chained to a prison wall during the fighting), and signed a treaty binding Algiers never again to engage in the enslavement of Christians. Exmouth had achieved complete success.

Unknown to its adversary, the Anglo-Dutch fleet was in fact in no position to renew the bombardment; the threat to do so amounted to nothing more than bluster. Exmouth's force had all but exhausted its supply of ammunition, having expended 118 tons (107 tonnes) of gunpowder and thousands of rounds of shot totalling 500 tons (454 tonnes) of iron. The *Queen Charlotte* alone had fired over 4,000 rounds, while the bomb vessels had hurled almost a thousand shells into the fortifications and city during the course of the fighting. There are no records of Algerine losses, but those for the British, which proved severe, are well-documented: 128 killed and 690 wounded – a total of 818 casualties, which represented 16 percent of Royal Navy personnel present that day, and a figure that exceeded the proportion of officers and seamen killed at any of the great battles fought by Nelson. The gallant *Impregnable*, which had occupied a perilous position in the harbor, was literally perforated, with 233 shot holes in her hull, and she had suffered 50 dead and 160 wounded. The Dutch took losses of 13 wounded and 52 killed. Total Anglo-Dutch casualties thus amounted to 180 killed and 703 wounded. The victory, though dearly bought, stands as a testament to Exmouth's meticulous preparation and planning, to his tactical brilliance, and, above all, to the technical expertise and fighting efficiency of his crews.

If, by force of arms, the long-standing practice of white slavery had at last been brought to a dramatic end, the piracy that had made it possible received only a temporary check. Sporadic acts of piracy continued for many years. In 1817, Tunisian corsairs ventured as far as the English Channel and the North Sea, taking vessels based at Hamburg and other north German ports, and as late as 1825 Sweden, Denmark, Portugal, and Naples were still paying annual tribute to some of the Barbary States. Even as late as 1827, Sweden continued to offer a token form of tribute consisting of 125 pieces of ordnance. But it was not to last, for a seemingly insignificant diplomatic incident occurred that same year whose consequences the Barbary States could neither foresee nor control.

French conquest and colonization

In April 1827 a dispute arose between the French consul and the dey of Algiers over the failure of the former, on his departure from the dey's presence, to use diplomatic language deemed sufficiently respectful. When the dey showed his displeasure by striking the consul with the handle of his fan, the French government refused to allow this insult to go unpunished, and accordingly dispatched a punitive expedition to Algiers. Yet the blockade imposed by the squadron deployed for the purpose proved so porous as to produce no effect except to annoy the dey, who retaliated by abusing the few French prisoners in his possession. The final affront came when, on ejecting a French diplomat from their capital in August 1829, the Algerines fired on his ship despite the presence of a flag of truce.

The French, determined to bring an end to the crisis, assembled a large fleet, commanded by Admiral Duperré, which left Toulon on May 26, 1830. This force sailed not simply to bombard Algiers, but to land 37,000 troops and 83 pieces of artillery under Marshal Louis Bourmont and occupy the city itself. The fleet arrived in a bay near Algiers on June 13, and on the following day disembarked its troops in the face of minor opposition. Six days later, after routing a force sent against him, Bourmont advanced inexorably on the city, forcing back all who sought to impede his progress. On July 4, the French began to bombard the city, the defenders blew up the magazine, the principal fort fell to the attackers, and the dey requested terms of surrender. When Bourmont guaranteed the safety of the dey

Bombardment of Algiers, August 27, 1816

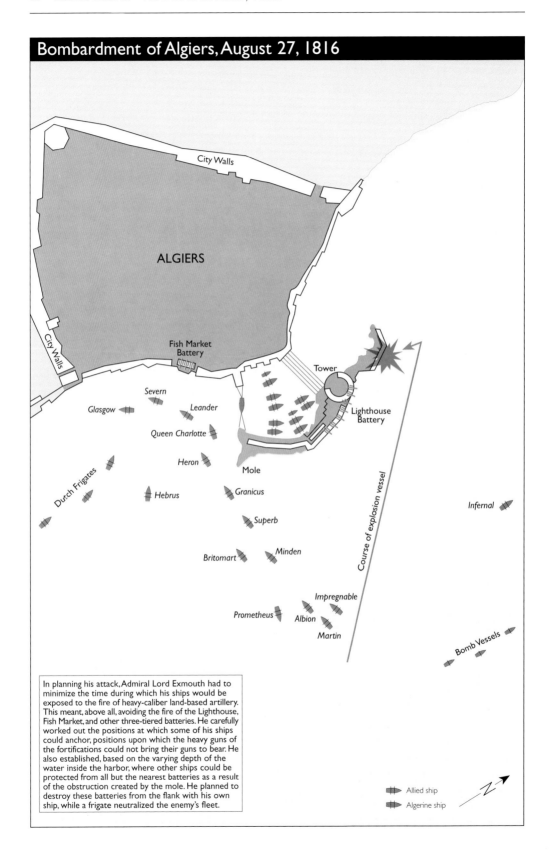

City Walls

ALGIERS

City Walls

Fish Market
Battery

Severn

Glasgow

Leander

Queen Charlotte

Heron

Dutch Frigates

Hebrus

Granicus

Superb

Britomart

Minden

Tower

Lighthouse
Battery

Mole

Course of explosion vessel

Infernal

Impregnable

Prometheus

Albion

Martin

Bomb Vessels

In planning his attack, Admiral Lord Exmouth had to minimize the time during which his ships would be exposed to the fire of heavy-caliber land-based artillery. This meant, above all, avoiding the fire of the Lighthouse, Fish Market, and other three-tiered batteries. He carefully worked out the positions at which some of his ships could anchor, positions upon which the heavy guns of the fortifications could not bring their guns to bear. He also established, based on the varying depth of the water inside the harbor, where other ships could be protected from all but the nearest batteries as a result of the obstruction created by the mole. He planned to destroy these batteries from the flank with his own ship, while a frigate neutralized the enemy's fleet.

Allied ship

Algerine ship

N

Exmouth's bombardment of Algiers, August 27, 1816. Engaging land-based fortifications with ships was no mean feat; the crews had to aim at the embrasures in an effort to disable the guns protruding through them, since fire directed against reinforced stonework generally produced poor results. (BHC0617; National Maritime Museum, London)

and the inhabitants of Algiers, the city capitulated, the French taking full possession on the 5th. The following week, a French frigate bearing the dey, his family, and possessions, sailed for Naples, thus bringing to a close the long chapter of Muslim rule over Algiers – and with it a permanent end to the centuries-old practice of piracy. Once in possession of Algiers, the French began expanding into the interior of the country and later across much of North Africa, so inaugurating a long, bloody war of conquest which did not end until December 1847.

French bombardment of Algiers, July 4, 1830. In seeking a permanent solution to the lingering problem of Barbary piracy, France also possessed a useful pretext for imperial expansion in North Africa. (PU0239; National Maritime Museum, London)

The Barbary Wars in perspective

If the history of America's relations with the Barbary States remains largely neglected, it is partly because unpalatable truths emerge when one begins to scratch the surface. The short-sighted policy that stripped the new nation of its navy left America prostrate at the feet of petty tyrants who could seize its citizens and reduce them to slavery with complete impunity. Thus, while many Americans, expressing a sense of righteous indignation, agreed with the cry of "Millions for defense, but not one penny for tribute!", successive administrations left American sailors to languish in captivity for a decade. Responsibility for this unsavory policy rests not with some long-forgotten, obscure president, but with no less than the iconic George Washington – hero of the Revolutionary War, founding father, and first president – under whose administration the United States became a tributary of the Barbary States. Even great men make mistakes; this, perhaps, was Washington's greatest.

There were, of course, mitigating factors at work. When seeking an explanation for America's initial failure to take a firm stand against the Barbary States, it is important to note that even after Decatur sailed into the ports of North Africa in 1815 to dictate peace, a century was still to pass before the United States entered the world stage. The fact that America has played a dominant part in global affairs since the Second World War must not be allowed to obscure the fact that two centuries ago it was a weak nation on the fringes of the international scene. As such, fresh from the Revolutionary War, the young republic had neither the financial resources nor the manpower to confront the menace of Barbary piracy. Seen in this light, the payment of ransom for the release of captives, together with annual tribute, was perhaps less short-sighted and morally

flawed than it might on the face of it appear, not least because the instinct to rescue fellow citizens from the horrors of slavery underpinned this policy.

Belatedly, the development of America's sense of national pride and dignity, backed by a small but efficient Navy, at last provided the United States with the means required for the new republic to achieve the full independence that had eluded it in 1783. For, objectively speaking, tributary nations by definition are not genuinely free.

Even when light is shone on this long-forgotten period, reality is occasionally distorted by those who would seek to satisfy a political agenda rather than establish historical fact. In no way is this more obviously so than with respect to the role – or lack thereof – played by religion in America's wars against the Barbary States. Despite the many parallels recently drawn between these conflicts and that between United States and al-Qaeda, the historical record does not lend itself to comparison. In short, the Barbary Wars did not constitute, as at least one author maintains, "America's first war on terror." America did not perceive itself at war with terrorists, however defined, and while piracy was clearly a scourge to American trade, the religious component to the wars was confined to the Barbary States' notion that Christians, being infidels, were inferior to Muslims. In recognizing this, one must not ignore the fact that, conversely, Christians felt themselves superior, morally and theologically speaking, to their Muslim opponents, as is clear from contemporary literature.

Yet however much the two sides condemned the other as deviants from the one true faith, they did not emphasize differences of religion in any more than peripheral terms – much less claim them as a motive for war. The Barbary States were not theocracies, with Muslim clerics controlling the levers of power. There was no "jihad," except insofar as the stirring of religious hatred served the interests of powers bent on profit. Nor had the United States, specifically founded on the basis of a separation of church and state, any religious agenda to pursue. It, too, sought profit, but in the form of free trade rather than piracy.

If a degree of hypocrisy creeps into the debate over the motives behind America's wars against the Barbary States, no more is this so than with respect to the issue of white slavery. Morally reprehensible though the enslavement of Christians by Muslims certainly was, it was no more unpalatable than the Western practice of enslaving black Africans. Slaves on American plantations had virtually no prospect of eventual release (known as manumission): they were denied citizenship, and their inferior status also denied them recourse to the judicial system to challenge the legal basis that categorized them as property rather than as people. Nor did sharing a common Christian faith – clearly interpreted differently by slaves and slave-owners – protect them from bondage.

By contrast, not only did the Barbary States decline to enslave co-religionists, they had a vested interest in releasing slaves, for freedom came at the price of ransom, for the purpose of which the captives had been taken in first place. If, pending their release, the white slaves held by the Barbary States were put to hard labor, poorly fed, and subjected to abuse, the same was true for slaves in South Carolina or Jamaica – the difference being that whereas a white slave in North Africa could hold out some hope of eventual release, the same could not be said for his black counterpart in North America. It is important, moreover, to compare the scale of slavery as practiced, for instance, in the United States on the one hand, and Algiers on the other. Whereas in 1790 there were nearly 700,000 slaves in America, there were only 3,000 in Algiers. Even an aggregate total for the whole of North Africa would not begin to approach the scale of slavery as conducted in the United States alone, not to mention the West Indies

and other parts of the New World. Western powers situated on the Atlantic seaboard, practically all of which themselves practiced slavery, naturally did not recognize this apparent paradox.

Nor can the Barbary practice of exacting tribute from enemies be condemned out of hand, for there are many contemporaneous examples of reparation payments exacted by European states. The French Revolutionary armies were notorious for requisitioning supplies on foreign soil, whether friend or foe; contributions were laid against most of the states France defeated, not least Prussia in 1807. The victorious Allies did the same, demanding financial compensation from France by the terms of the Second Treaty of Paris in 1815, which authorized troops to remain in occupation until France fulfilled its obligations. Where actual cash did not change hands, territory certainly did, which amounted to much the same thing.

If the Barbary Wars raise some contentious issues, with motives sometimes misrepresented, false parallels drawn, and hypocrisies exposed, it is important to look beyond the peripheral issues to reveal the broad historical significance of these conflicts. In strictly military and naval terms, the Barbary Wars form but a footnote in the historiography of war; yet even a small conflict can produce a lasting impact out of all proportion to its size. No more is this so than with respect to the United States. The Barbary Wars not only ended America's status as a tributary to the petty states of North Africa, they also enabled the United States to regain its sense of national dignity, and permanently demolished the short-sighted notion that America – a nation still effectively confined to the Atlantic seaboard and utterly dependent on the freedom of the seas – could function without a proper navy to protect that freedom.

But if for the United States the Barbary Wars were principally about the protection of its trade and of its citizens, they also functioned as a catalyst for the development of a navy that in time would grow to become an important instrument of American

foreign policy. Further, if the impending war with France in 1798 led directly to the formal establishment of the Department of the Navy and to a gratifying string of ship-to-ship victories, the Barbary Wars enabled that same, more experienced, navy to function as a cohesive fighting force – as a proper squadron and to contribute substantially to its growing self-confidence. In this small yet significant fashion, only 20 years after independence, the United States was already projecting its newly acquired power thousands of miles across the Atlantic.

By contemporary European standards that power was pathetically small, but the salient point remains: the significance of the naval squadron in the Mediterranean lay not in the crude calculation of ships and guns, but in its mere *presence*, for it symbolized America's determination to pursue its interests wherever it saw fit. Only

Nomads and their black slaves caught in a violent sand storm. Mathew Carey, a former American captive, cogently exposed his country's hypocritical attitude towards slavery: "For this practice … we are not entitled to charge the Algerines with any exclusive degree of barbarity. The Christians of Europe and America carry on this commerce an [sic] hundred times more extensively than the Algerines." (New York Public Library Picture Collection)

a few years later, the Navy more than answered the country's expectations in the war against Britain, and by the time Decatur sailed into Algiers in 1815 to dictate peace "at the mouths of cannon," the United States bore the unmistakable marks of a nation destined to play a major role in international affairs.

Thus, the earliest origins of America's now pre-eminent position on the world stage may be traced back well before the world wars – to the moment the Stars and Stripes began to flutter in the wind "on the shores of Tripoli."

Further reading

Alden, Carroll Storrs, and Ralph Earle. *Makers of Naval Tradition*. New York: Gin and Co., 1942

Allen, Gardner W. *Our Navy and the Barbary Corsairs*. Cranbury, NJ: The Scholar's Bookshelf, 2005 (originally published in 1905 by Houghton Mifflin)

Allison, Robert J. *The Crescent Obscured: The United States and the Muslim World, 1776–1815*. Chicago: University of Chicago Press, 2000

Allison, Robert J. *Stephen Decatur: American Naval Hero, 1779–1820*. Boston: University of Massachusetts Press, 2005

Ambrose, Stephen. *Undaunted Courage: Meriwether Lewis, Thomas Jefferson, and the Opening of the American West*. New York: Simon and Schuster, 1997

Baepler, Paul, ed. *White Slaves, African Masters: An Anthology of American Barbary Captivity Narratives*. Chicago: University of Chicago Press, 1999

Carey, Matthew. *A Short Account of Algiers, Containing a Description of the climate of That Country, of the Manners and Inhabitants ... with a concise View of the Origins of the Rupture between Algiers and the United States*. Philadelphia: 1794

Chidsey, Donald Barr. *The Wars in Barbary: Arab Piracy and the Birth of the United States Navy*. New York: Crown, 1971

Clowes, William Laird. *The Royal Navy: A History from Earliest Times to 1900*. 7 vols, Vol. 6. London: Chatham Publishing, 1997

Davis, Robert C. *Christian Slaves, Muslim Masters: White Slavery in the Mediterranean, the Barbary Coast and Italy, 1500–1800*. London: Palgrave Macmillan, 2004

Dearden, Seton. *A Nest of Corsairs: The Fighting Karamanlis of Tripoli*. London: John Murray, 1976

de Kay, James Tertius. *A Rage for Glory: The Life of Commodore Stephen Decatur, USN*. New York: The Free Press, 2004

de Selding, Charles. *Documents, Official and Unofficial, Relating to the Case of the Capture and Destruction of the Frigate* Philadelphia, *at Tripoli, on the 16th of February, 1804*. Washington, DC: J.T. Towers, 1850

Edwards, Samuel (also under the pseudonym Noel Gershon). *Barbary General: The Life of William H. Eaton*. Englewood Cliffs, NJ: Prentice-Hall, 1968

Ferguson, Eugene S. *Truxton of the "Constellation": The Life of Commodore Thomas Truxton, U.S. Navy, 1755–1822*. Baltimore, MD: The Johns Hopkins University Press, 2001

Field, James A. *America and the Mediterranean World, 1776–1882*. Princeton, NJ: Princeton University Press, 1969

Fisher, Sir Godfrey. *Barbary Legend: War, Trade and Piracy in North Africa, 1415–1830*. Oxford: Clarendon Press, 1957

Footner, Geoffrey M. *USS* Constellation: *From Frigate to Sloop of War*. Annapolis, MD: Naval Institute Press, 2002

Forester, C.S. *The Barbary Pirates*. New York: Random House, 1953

Foss, John. *A Journal of the Captivity and Sufferings of John Foss; several years a prisoner in Algiers*. Newburyport, MA: A. March, 1798

Fowler, William M., Jr. *Jack Tars and Commodores: The American Navy, 1783–1815*. Boston: Houghton Mifflin, 1984

Gruppe, Henry. *The Frigates*. Alexandria, VA: Time-Life Books, 1980

Guttridge, Leonard F., and Jay D. Smith. *The Commodores: The U.S. Navy in the Age of Sail*. New York: Harper and Row, 1969

Guttridge, Leonard. *Our Country Right or Wrong: The Life and Times of Stephen Decatur*. New York: Forge Books, 2006

Heers, Jacques. *The Barbary Corsairs: Warfare in the Mediterranean, 1480–1580*. London: Greenhill, 2003

Irwin, Ray W. *The Diplomatic Relations of the United States with the Barbary Powers, 1776–1816*. Chapel Hill: University of North Carolina Press, 1931

Julien, Charles-André. *History of North Africa*. New York: Praeger Publishers, 1970

Kitzen, Michael L. *Tripoli and the United States at War: A History of American Relations with the Barbary States, 1785–1805*. Jefferson, NC: McFarland & Co., 1993

Lambert, Frank. *The Barbary Wars: American Independence in the Atlantic World*. New York: Hill and Wang, 2005

Lane-Poole, Stanley. *The Barbary Corsairs*. London: T. Fisher, 1890

Lardas, Mark. *American Heavy Frigates, 1794–1826*. Oxford: Osprey, 2003

Leiner, Frederick C. *Millions for Defense: The Subscription Warships of 1798*. Annapolis, MD: Naval Institute Press, 2000

Leiner, Frederick C. *The End of Barbary Terror: America's 1815 War Against the Pirates of North Africa*. New York: Oxford University Press, 2006

London, Joshua. *Victory in Tripoli: How America's War with the Barbary Pirates established the U.S. Navy and Shaped a Nation*. Hoboken, NJ: John Wiley & Sons, 2005

Long, David F. *Ready to Hazard: A Biography of Commodore William Bainbridge, 1774–1833*. Hanover, NH: University Press of New England, 1981

Mackenzie, Alexander Slidell. *The Life of Stephen Decatur, a Commodore in the Navy of the United States*. Boston: C.C. Little & J. Brown, 1846

Martin, Tyrone. *A Most Fortunate Ship: A Narrative History of Old Ironsides*. Annapolis, MD: Naval Institute Press, 1997

McKee, Christopher. *Edward Preble: A Naval Biography, 1761–1807*. Annapolis, MD: Naval Institute Press, 1972

McKee, Christopher. *A Gentlemanly and Honorable Profession: The Creation of the U.S. Naval Officer Corps, 1794–1815*. Annapolis, MD: Naval Institute Press, 1991

Milton, Giles. *White Gold: The Extraordinary Story of Thomas Pellow and Islam's One Million White Slaves*. London: Hodder & Stoughton, 2005

Moulton, Gary E. *The Lewis and Clark Journals: An American Epic of Discovery*. Lincoln, NE: University of Nebraska Press, 2003

Nicholson, Thomas. *An Affecting Narrative of the Captivity and Sufferings of Thomas Nicholson … Who has been Six Years a Prisoner among the Algerines, and from whom he fortunately made his escape a few months previous to Commodore Decatur's late Expedition*. Boston: H. Trumbull, 1816

Panzac, Daniel. *The Barbary Corsairs: The End of a Legend, 1800–1820*. Boston: Brill Academic Publishers, 2004

Parker, Richard. *Uncle Sam in Barbary: A Diplomatic History*. Tallahassee: University Press of Florida, 2004

Perkins, Kenneth. *On the Eve of Colonialism: North Africa Before the French Conquest, 1790–1830*. New York: Holmes and Meier, 1977 (A translation of Valensi, Lucette. *Le Maghreb avant la prise d'Alger*. Paris: Flammarion, 1969)

Perkins, Roger. *Gunfire in Barbary: Admiral Lord Exmouth's battle with the Corsairs of Algiers in 1816*. Emsworth, UK: K. Mason, 1982

Pratt, Fletcher. *Preble's Boys: Commodore Preble and the Birth of American Sea Power*. New York: William Sloane Associates, 1950

Ray, William. *Horrors of Slavery; or, American Tars in Tripoli*. Troy, NY: Oliver Lyon, 1808

Seaton, Dearborn. *A Nest of Corsairs: The Fighting Karamanlis on the Barbary Coast*. London: John Murray, 1976

Silverstone, Paul H. *The Sailing Navy, 1775–1854*. Annapolis, MD: Naval Institute Press, 2001

Smelser, Marshall. *The Congress Founds the Navy, 1787–1798*. South Bend, IN: Notre Dame University Press, 1959

Spencer, William. *Algiers in the Age of the Corsairs*. Norman, OK: University of Oklahoma Press, 1976

Tubbs, Stephenie Ambrose and Clay Jenkinson. *The Lewis and Clark Companion: An Encyclopedic Guide to the Voyage of Discovery*. New York: Owl Books, 2003

Tucker, Glenn. *Dawn Like Thunder: The Barbary Wars and the Birth of the U.S. Navy*. Indianapolis, IN: Bobbs-Merrill, 1963

Tucker, Spencer. *Stephen Decatur: A Life Most Bold and Daring*. Annapolis, MD: Naval Institute Press, 2005

Tully, Richard. *Narrative of Ten Years' Residence at Tripoli*. London: Arthur Barker, 1957 (originally published in London by Coburn, 1819)

United States. Department of the Navy. *Naval Documents Related to the United States Wars with the Barbary Powers: Naval Operations Including Diplomatic Background, 1785–1807*. 6 vols, ed. Dudley W. Knox. Washington, DC: US Government Printing Office, 1939–44

Waldo, Putnam S. *The Life and Character of Stephen Decatur*. Whitefish, MO: Kessinger, 2004

Wheelan, Joseph. *Jefferson's War: America's First War on Terror, 1801–1805*. New York: Carroll & Graf, 2004

Whipple, A.B.C. *To the Shores of Tripoli: The Birth of the U.S. Navy and Marines*. Annapolis, MD: Naval Institute Press, 1991

Wolf, John. *The Barbary Coast: Algiers under the Turks, 1500–1830*. New York, W.W. Norton & Co., 1979

Wright, Louis and Julia Macleod. *The First Americans in North Africa: William Eaton's Struggle for a Vigorous Policy against the Barbary Pirates, 1792–1805*. Princeton, NJ: Princeton University Press, 1945

Zacks, Richard. *The Pirate Coast: Thomas Jefferson, The First Marines, and the Secret Mission of 1805*. New York: Hyperion, 2005

Index

Visit the Osprey website

- Information about forthcoming books

- Author information

- Read extracts and see sample pages

- Sign up for our free newsletters

- Competitions and prizes

www.ospreypublishing.com